COLORFUL COLORADO

D0111307

Louise Pote

The Author

Caroline Bancroft is a third generation Coloradan who began writing her first history for The Denver Post in 1928.

Her long-standing interest in western history was inherited. Her pioneer grandfather, Dr. F. J. Bancroft, was a founder of the Colorado Historical Society and its first president.

His granddaughter has carried on the family tradition. She is the author of the interesting series of Bancroft Booklets, *Silver Queen: The Fabulous Story of Baby Doe Tabor, Famous Aspen, Denver's Lively Past, Historic Central City, The Brown Palace in Denver, Tabor's Matchless Mine and Lusty Leadville, Augusta Tabor: Her Side of the Scandal, The Unsinkable Mrs. Brown, Glenwood's Early Glamor, Colorado's Lost Gold Mines, Unique Ghost Towns, Six Racy Madams of Colorado,* and *Estes Park and Grand Lake.*

A Bachelor of Arts from Smith College, she later obtained a Master of Arts degree from the University of Denver, writing her thesis on Central City, Colorado. Her full-size *Gulch of Gold* is the definitive, but very popular, history of that well-known area.

STEPHEN L. R. McNICHOLS
Governor of Colorado
1956-1962

The above photo was taken at the Mother Cabrini Shrine above Mt. Vernon Canyon which is a national mecca for Catholics. In the background is the continental divide with three-crested Mt. Bancroft, named for the author's grandfather, showing.

Cover: Mount Sneffels near Ouray, Colorado. Photo courtesy of State of Colorado Division of Commerce and Development.

COLORFUL COLORADO

Its Dramatic History

by

CAROLINE BANCROFT

JOHNSON BOOKS
Boulder, Colorado

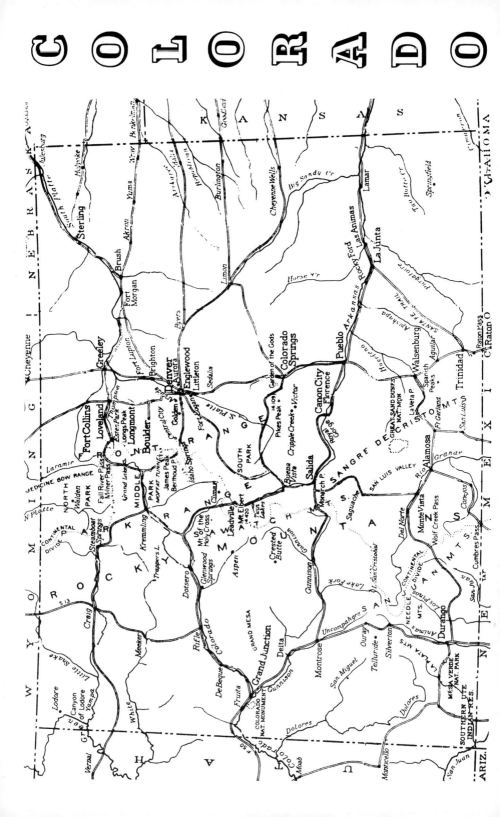

COLORFUL COLORADO

Colorado is a Spanish word. It means reddish, rosy or colorful and was given to the land that later became the state of Colorado by the early Spanish explorers. As the conquistadores rode along on that fearsome animal, the horse, new to North American Indians, they saw many different red rock formations—sometimes geologic layers of sandstone, sometimes erosion remnants or cliffs, sometimes whole mountains of red rock. Naturally they thought of the region as "colorado."

And "colorado," or colorful, it is. The whole region abounds in color. In the eastern part of the state waving stands of golden wheat or green fields filled with clumps of sugar beets vie with the red and white of Hereford cattle as the herds munch prairie grasses. Toward the center of the state the pine-green rampart of the Rocky Mountains, topped by the snow-crested continental divide, rises up to over fourteen thousand feet with fifty-four peaks passing that mark. In the western section castellated mesas, dramatic canyons, black gorges and high blue lakes paint every scene in striking hues. The state is almost too colorful for an artist's palette.

Its history shows a like pattern. Many colorful events have followed each other down the centuries to make up the story of Colorado. Most of these events have been dramatic, and, although others have been sombre, the over-all pageant that they created is one where kaleidoscopic scenes predominate in a changing tale.

The tale's beginnings are in the long, long ago—some fifteen thousand years ago—and are obscured by the mists of time. Despite the fact that Coloradans are in the habit of thinking of their history as slightly more than a century old (because Spanish-American settlements in the San Luis Valley began in the early 1850's and Anglo-American towns along the borders of the Front Range toward the last of the same decade), the story really began with prehistoric beings called Folsom Man.

These early men are known to us only through artifacts that they left when they inhabited this region. In the twentieth century, thousands of years later, their human products were found in geologically-formed rock layers of the earth and dug up by archeologists who then reconstructed the life of Folsom Man. He lived on bison, camels, and mammoths which he killed with a lance and arrow. These animals have long been extinct, but some of their skeletons, imbedded with the lanceheads that wounded them, were preserved in perfect fossil form. The discovery of these fossils graphically illustrated Folsom Man's life.

One site, so rich in fossils and artifacts that it proved to be an actual home or village of these early people, was on the Lindenmeier ranch north of Fort Collins. From 1934 to 1940 the Smithsonian Institution of Washington, D. C., conducted seven seasons of excavations at this site trying to probe the final mystery of man's prehistoric life. Archeologists unearthed stone lanceheads (hand scraped to the shape known as Folsom Points), stone scrapers, stone blades, stone beads for adornment and carved bone fragments, but curiously no remnant of Folsom Man himself. Perhaps he had some special burial custom, at a distance from his habitation, which might account for there being no trace of his own skeletons with the artifacts. But the mystery was never solved.

We do know that he lived a dangerous life, harassed by gigantic beasts and terrified by geologic activity. The region of the Rockies was still boiling up with volcanic and igneous intrusions in fiery periods that alternated with cold cycles when successive flows of ice and glaciers swept down the canyons and valleys. It is remarkable that any trace at all of Folsom Man survived these holocausts.

The next group of men came much later and apparently inhabited the Colorado region from around 700 A.D. to 1000 A.D. They were a very primitive Indian tribe who knew nothing about agriculture and ate roots, berries, seeds and insects, or whatever wild life they could catch by hand, since they had no weapons. No doubt doves, prairie dogs, and rabbits sometimes were slaughtered to enhance the bill of fare. These earliest Indians probably lived in cone-shaped brush houses, called wickiups, which could be easily assembled. Since they were always in search of food, they were forced to be roamers.

Far to the south of them were peoples who were more advanced. In Mexico the Indians had discovered the worth of corn and how to grow it. Gradually this knowledge, accompanied by seed, worked its way northward and changed the nomads of the Colorado region into farmers. Now the primitive Indians did not have to roam.

They looked about for a safe place to live, close to easily tillable fields, and hit upon the idea of carving out apartment houses in cliffs. They soon developed a series of these unique habitations, of which the

6

THE CLIFF DWELLERS MOVED ON TOP

As these peaceful Indians grew strong and unafraid, they built new high homes like the above—Far View House. (See color illustrations also.)

Cliff Palace in the Mesa Verde National Park is the most elaborate and well-known sample. But remains of their communal residences may be found elsewhere in southwest Colorado as well as in the northwest section of the state. All the tribes were a cliff dwelling people.

The Cliff Dwellers flourished from around 1050 A.D. to 1250 A.D., a period in Europe that embraced the Norman conquest and the Crusades. Their history fell into two successive periods, described as the Basketmaker and the Pueblo, so divided because of the difference in the skeletons, skulls, and tools dug up from the ruins.

The Basketmakers were a squat people, whose expert weaving was the basis of their culture. They were able to make baskets of such fine, tight texture that the baskets would hold water or could be used as cooking utensils by dropping hot stones in them. Although the Basketmakers could not read nor write and had no horses, cattle or sheep, they were fine farmers and good builders.

They used stone hammers to square building blocks and stone axes to fell pine and cedar for use as beams. They had to drag these materials by hand to the site of their residences because they had no knowledge of wheels for hand carts or wheelbarrows. Yet even with these primitive methods they and their successors, the Pueblans, were able to complete great community houses that have stood for nearly nine centuries snugly fitted into cliffs and approachable only by ladders that could be drawn up for protection from their enemies. The buildings were both utilitarian and complex. In the Cliff Palace alone there are over one hundred living rooms in addition to twenty-three kivas. (These were circular underground rooms used for secret religious activities, and as club rooms for the men and boys).

The Pueblans were taller and had a flat skull at the back (probably the result of strapping papooses to flat boards). Their increased height

7

has led archeologists to think that new people came into the region at this time and intermarried with the original Basketmakers. No exact demarcation can be made between the two periods but in general the Pueblans were more skilled craftsmen. They developed the art of pottery, which the Basketmakers had discovered, to a high degree.

In the earlier stages the bowls and pots were very crude, mostly undecorated and simply made from dark grey or red clay. The Pueblans carried this craft forward until it became a beautiful art with many striking black-on-white designs. They also introduced the bow and arrow, cotton, beans, and turkeys. As they expanded and prospered, they felt strong enough to move up on top of the mesa and to construct large communal houses away from the protection of the cliffs. Far View House in the Mesa Verde National Park is the best known of these structures.

The mats, baskets, spears, pottery, blankets, bows and arrows, sandals, and other implements and household goods which were left by both divisions of Cliff Dwellers prove that they were accomplished workmen. They were a peaceful people and developed an apparently democratic form of government as well as a ceremonial religion. Their degree of civilization is attested to by the remains of carefully-engineered irrigation ditches, built even before the principle of irrigation had moved from Egypt to Europe.

And then the Cliff Dwellers disappeared. What happened to them? No one knows for certain. The most logical assumption is that they were killed off by a twenty-three year drought which lasted from 1276 to 1299. The actuality of this drought has been established by A. E. Douglas of Arizona in his study of tree rings, and it seems probable that a people, dependent upon farming, could not survive such a disaster. Their crops would have dried up and they would either have starved or been forced to leave their fields for new lands.

In succeeding centuries nomadic Indians, like the Utes and Comanches in the mountains and the Arapahoes and the Cheyennes on the plains, took over the land of Colorado. Their civilization was a more primitive one than that of the Cliff Dwellers. It was based on hunting small animals and deer, elk, antelope, and coyotes with the bow and arrow. But particularly they hunted the buffalo. The Indians killed this large prey by driving the animals over cliffs, crippling them, and clubbing them to death, since bows and arrows were ineffectual against their tough hides except at very close range.

The buffalo, or American bison, grazed during those centuries in countless numbers throughout the eastern plains and in many mountain grasslands such as South Park. Although the animal's powerful frame

CORONADO CAME RIDING ON A WHITE HORSE

*When the Spanish invaded the Southwest in 1540 and crossed Colorado
the next year, they astounded the Plains Indians by riding strange beasts.*

and speed made it difficult for an Indian on foot to best him, yet he had
to do it, since the buffalo's carcass meant complete existence for the red
man. The hide made tepees for shelter and garments to wear; the fur
provided robes to sleep on; the flesh and entrails gave the Indian food;
the muscles made bowstrings and lacings; and the horns and hooves
could be fashioned into utensils. The buffalo was the Indian's very life.

Then, in the sixteenth century, the Indians who were living in the
region of Colorado entered into a dashing new phase with the advent of
the white man. When the Spaniards under Coronado arrived in the
Southwest from Mexico City during 1540, a strange terrifying animal
accompanied the conquistadores, an animal that was to influence the
whole Rocky Mountain and plains culture. This was the horse. Transportation, hunting and raiding acquired a new ease with horses as
beasts of burden, as means of pursuit of the buffalo, and as a method of
maneuverability in warfare.

Coronado did not come exploring with any such result in mind. His
idea was to conquer the land and to obtain gold. His mounted troops
pranced northward, with shining armor, silver-mounted trappings, and
gaily colored banners, to find the mythical land of Quivira and the
Seven Cities of Cibola. There, so the alluring rumors ran, the inhabitants ate from solid gold utensils, and the streets were paved with the
gleaming metal.

The Spaniards were doomed to disappointment and disaster. When
Coronado first came into sight of the Pueblo Indian villages of the Rio
Grande (in the region of the present cities of Albuquerque and Santa
Fe), their terraced adobe bulk was shining in the distant sunlight (the

9

luminosity perhaps heightened by mica flakes). Coronado was sure that he had arrived at the end of his quest. But as he neared the poverty-stricken, mud-walled settlements, his disillusionment was profound. These villages were not the Seven Cities of Cibola and the inhabitants knew nothing of gold.

The Indians (who were no doubt anxious to get rid of the terrifying foreigners) said that Quivira, the other mythical place that Coronado sought, was farther on—over in Kansas.

So the Spaniards pushed eastward, amazed at hordes of the "hump-backed cow"—the buffalo—which they later described to European audiences. But when after many hardships they reached Kansas, there was no gold. Weary, dispirited, and now starving, they straggled back across the plains and probably through the southeastern corner of Colorado. If that was their route, they were the first white men to touch the state's soil and to see the grandeur of the vast Colorado grasslands. But there was no grandeur for them—only disgrace, when they returned to Mexico City. Their avowed mission of "Gold, Glory and Gospel" had miserably failed.

The Spanish influence on the state, except for the horses they lost or traded for food and which later multiplied, was of no importance during the period of this expedition nor during the century that followed. Although the Spanish were becoming entrenched in Mexico and in the Southwest, it was not until over a hundred years later, sometime between 1664 and 1680, that Colorado soil was so much as touched by the boots of a white man. In the intervening time the Spanish had enslaved the Indians of New Mexico and imposed harsh taxes. In desperation a band

HORSES MADE LIFE EASIER FOR THE INDIANS

Some of the Spanish horses escaped and were captured by the Indians who soon learned to train them. Here the horses are pulling travois.

of Indians from Taos fled to a place some hundred miles east of present Pueblo and there fortified themselves at a spot called Cuartelejo. The Spanish governor sent a military expedition of twenty white soldiers and a force of Indian auxiliaries after them. It was captained by Juan Archuleta who pursued the fugitives, captured them and returned them to Taos.

In 1680 the Pueblo Indians of New Mexico under Pope, a medicine man, united against the Spaniards and drove the invaders back to El Paso. But twelve years later, in 1692, Diego de Vargas led an expedition up the Rio Grande to retake the territory. He was successful in his reconquest, but in the succeeding years many of the Indians refused to supply rations to the militant Spanish. With food running short, de Vargas decided to conduct a campaign against some of the Indian pueblos north of Santa Fe in an effort to obtain corn. The Indians were in a rebellious mood and planned to ambush de Vargas and his men on their way back to Santa Fe. The Spanish heard of this plan and decided on a roundabout route home.

They pushed north into the San Luis valley and on July 8, 1694, camped on the Culebra River, in present Costilla County. The next day they found a ford over the Rio Grande and came upon a herd of five hundred buffalo grazing in a meadow. They were able to gain a large supply of meat and to sneak down the west side of the Rio Grande, thus outwitting the plan of the New Mexico Indians. A band of Colorado Utes started to attack their camp one day, mistaking the expedition for one of enemy Pueblo Indians. When the Utes discovered that the intruders were Spanish, a friendly powwow was held, and de Vargas invited the Utes to come to Santa Fe to trade as they had done before the Pope uprising. He was in a pleasant mood with ample food for many months.

But in the following years "Gold, Glory and Gospel" continued to be the slogan of the Spaniards and they were ruthless in their emphasis on all three. Soon it was not only the Pueblo Indians that were resentful but also the neighboring tribes that touched on the Spanish domain, particularly the Comanches in Colorado.

Cruel and domineering, the Spanish sowed seeds which caused trouble between the white man and the red for centuries. The injustices committed by the intruders provoked retaliation from the Indians. Each side tried to outdo the other in barbarities. The northern Indians would swoop out of Colorado upon the white settlements in the upper Rio Grande valley of New Mexico, fire the houses, scalp the farmers, and drive off the horses; or the Pueblo Indians would run away from slavery under the Spaniards in New Mexico to seek a refuge in Colorado. Then

11

the Spaniards would retaliate with an expedition sent northward to punish the mountain Indians or retrieve the Pueblan slaves. Colorado became a battlefield.

One of these Spanish expeditions northward ocurred in 1706 and proved momentous. Juan de Ulibarri, with forty soldiers and a hundred Indian allies, led another slave-capturing expedition to El Cuartelejo, the fortified place east of Pueblo in Colorado. It was at this time that the Spaniards officially claimed the country in the name of their king despite the fact that the Indians contended that the land belonged to them. Ulibarri wrote a report of this first recorded claim to Colorado soil and reported the ceremony of formal possession in these words:

"The royal ensign Don Francisco de Valdez drew his sword, and I, after making a note of the events of the day and hour on which we arrived, said in a clear intelligible voice: 'Knights, Companions and Friends: Let the broad new province of San Luis and the great settlement of Santo Domingo of El Cuartelejo be pacified by the arms of us who are the vassals of our monarch, king and natural lord, Don Philip V—may he live forever.' The royal ensign said: 'Is there any one to contradict?' All responded, 'No.' Then he said: 'Long live the king! Long live the king! Long live the king!' and cutting the air in all four directions with his sword the ensign signalled for the discharge of the guns. After throwing up our hats and making other signs of rejoicing, the ceremony came to an end."

While the Spanish were claiming the land in colorful formal ceremonies and the Indians were resentfully combating their ownership, a third contender arrived to confuse the issue even further. Some years before, the French had settled in Canada and the Great Lakes region. When La Salle floated down the Mississippi in 1682, he claimed the entire territory drained by the "Father-of-Waters" for France in a formal declaration "in the name of the most high, mighty, invincible, and victorious Prince, Louis the great, by the grace of God, King of France and Navarre, Fourteenth of that name." Soon other Frenchmen set out to explore the headwaters of their nation's new acquisition and moved closer and closer to the land where the Spanish were entrenched.

The Spanish authorities in Santa Fe, jealous of their prerogatives as first-comers to Colorado, sent an expedition under Pedro de Villasur in 1720 into the eastern part of the state to defend their rights. But Villasur's troop of more than one hundred Spaniards was ambushed by the Indians on the South Platte River. Probably the Indians were led by Frenchmen, but in any case the ambush efficiently ended Spain's claims to eastern Colorado. The defenders slaughtered all but six of Villasur's men, who fled, wounded and frightened, back to the safety of Santa Fe.

France continued to advance in America, not only geographically, but also in amity and trade with the natives. The French were already set upon a course of intermarriage and friendship that would never cause serious trouble with the Indians. Their methods were the direct opposite of those of the Spanish, English, and, later, the Americans. (It is perhaps not amiss to observe that in the next century Canada, which profited by French teachings, had no uprisings or massacres during the same periods that the United States was racked with Indian troubles.) But at this time, the early 1700's, neither Canada nor the United States existed, and the French progressed steadily up the waterways toward the Rockies.

The particular French who traveled along the Platte River toward the boundaries of Colorado were the Mallet brothers, Peter and Paul, and six companions. In the year 1739 they gave the stream its name, Platte, probably because they had attempted to use a platte, a flat-bottomed river boat, to navigate or ford the river. After following the river for a considerable length of time, to a point somewhere between the present sites of Columbus and Grand Island, Nebraska, they crossed the river and moved in a southwesterly direction until they encountered the Arkansas, west of the Big Bend, in present Kansas. They threaded their way up this river to either the Purgatoire River or Timpas Creek, followed the waterway to the present site of Trinidad, and thence over Raton Pass to Santa Fe. (The Mallets were the first to lay out a route

THE SPANISH REMEMBERED THEIR RULERS

The Spanish Peaks, Ferdinand and Isabella, known for their beauty and prominence, are close to Walsenburg southeast of La Veta Pass.

THE BRAVES HUNTED BUFFALO WITH LANCES

Horses made killing buffalo an exciting pursuit instead of a grim necessity, except, of course, when a big bull turned to fight and gore his foe.

through Colorado, which is now traveled regularly, over two centuries later, by the Santa Fe Railroad's Super Chief streamliner.) After spending the winter in Santa Fe, the Mallets returned to French Louisiana by way of the Canadian river and so did not again touch the land of Colorado.

The Mallet expedition was the forerunner of several French trading missions to New Spain in the next fifteen years. These travelers had no delusions of "gold, glory or gospel." They were adventurous traders, intent on one thing only—business. But the Spaniards were alarmed by their enterprise and treated them coldly. New Spain refused to trade with the French.

Unfortunately just at this time, France became embroiled in that misnamed war, the French-Indian. This was actually a contest between England and France to determine which empire was to be allowed to expand in America. When the English won, France retired from the American colonial scene and in 1763 ceded all the land that is now eastern Colorado to Spain as England's ally. Without lifting her finger in America, Spain was the victor and became the owner of the entire state of Colorado.

But Spain was not interested in the vast prairie lands east of the Rockies so there was comparatively little activity there. It was different in the mountainous section. Because the Spanish were concerned about Russian expansion down the Pacific coastline from Alaska, they wanted to find a more direct route from Santa Fe to the new Spanish colony of San Francisco. The Spanish authorities dispatched two famous padres,

14

THE SQUAWS WORKED HARD ON THE CARCASSES

Squaws skinned the beasts and dressed the meat and hides while ponies and braves rested after the hunt. Some men cut choice slices to eat raw.

Dominguez and Escalante, and eight lay companions to explore the Colorado Rockies.

Today many of our place names in the southwestern part of the state date from this expedition. The party set out in July, 1776, the same time that the American Revolution was flaring up on the Atlantic seaboard. Fray Escalante was a meticulous journal-keeper who worked very closely with the map-maker of the party. For the first time in history a serious account, covering a section of present-day Colorado, was committed to paper.

Because of Father Escalante's journal the expedition is most frequently called by his name, although Father Dominguez was the technical leader. The party encountered such villainous terrain that they were unable to reach their goal, San Francisco. They explored the major portion of western Colorado, including parts of the stream beds of the Los Pinos, Animas, Dolores, San Miguel, Uncompahgre, Gunnison, Colorado, and White Rivers. They entered Utah, crossed the Green River, and continued on to the Wasatch Mountains. On October 6 snow fell and the disheartened padres decided to abandon their original purpose. They turned south, found their way into Arizona, crossed New Mexico, and reached their home base of Santa Fe early in January, 1777.

Santa Fe was still the capital for the New Mexico province of New Spain, but its tenure was a harassed and precarious one. During the entire century prior to the Escalante expedition troubles with the Indians had increased. The Comanche Indians, who inhabited moun-

15

ZEBULON PIKE

First official explorer of Colorado, prior to the gold rush period, was a lieutenant, when assigned to lead his troop west. He steadily rose in rank until at the time of his death he was a brigadier-general. He died a hero's death in the War of 1812 at the Battle of York when the U. S. besieged Toronto. Pike was but thirty-four. He had only six years to forge his fame.

tainous Colorado, grew bolder and more successful with each successive raid on the Spanish. They killed sheep and herders, and captured women, children, and horses. Punitive expeditions by the Spanish sometimes recovered stock but were only partially successful. Finally in 1778 vigorous Juan Bautista de Anza, founder of San Francisco, arrived in Santa Fe, having been appointed Governor of New Mexico the year before. He found conditions almost desperate and led a force of six hundred Spaniards into Colorado to teach a severe lesson to the Comanches and their bold Chief Greenhorn.

Anza was successful in his campaign. Aided by Ute and Arapaho braves, he defeated the Comanches in a series of battles. Anza killed Chief Greenhorn on Greenhorn Creek at the base of Greenhorn Mountain, which take their names from this incident. Following his eight-hundred-and-seventy-mile journey into Colorado with its smashing victories, general peace with the Indians was established for a number of years.

But at the turn of the century a momentous occurrence altered Spain's course in the new world. In 1800 Napoleon induced Spain to cede back the great Louisiana Territory to France, and then in 1803 France sold it to the United States. Inasmuch as the actual boundaries of the Louisiana Territory on the eastern slope of the Rockies were not established, the sale led to friction and distrust between Spain and the United States. Colorado, from the continental divide eastward, was considered in the Louisiana Territory by France; but Spain contended that her land extended north to the Arkansas River. This controversy lasted until

JOHN GUNNISON

Last official explorer before the gold rush period was a captain who had served the U. S. Topographical Engineers ever since his graduation from West Point. He had aided in moving the Cherokees west from Florida and in mapping the Great Salt Lake region besides other unexplored parts. He was forty-one years old when Indians killed him.

1819 when the question was finally settled and the boundary lines agreed upon. But in the interim the disputed land was dangerous territory.

The first act of the United States was to send explorers afield to find out what the government had bought. Not only were the boundary lines vague but no adequate knowledge existed of the geography of the land. First the Lewis and Clark expedition was dispatched across the continent by way of the Missouri in 1804. Later they were followed by Zebulon Montgomery Pike who was directed to explore the source of the Mississippi in 1805. When this mission was successful, the next year he was ordered to go up the Arkansas to explore the southern part of the Louisiana Purchase.

Lieutenant Pike's band of twenty-two men began their journey of discovery on July 15, 1806, garbed in summer uniforms and inadequately equipped for their rigorous undertaking. It took them until November 12 to touch the eastern border of Colorado and until November 24 to reach what they thought mistakenly was the base of the peak later to bear the name of the twenty-seven-year-old captain. (Pike was promoted in August.) The party failed to climb the peak and went on to still other failures. The disastrous results and mysterious happenings of the trip have supplied historians ever since with points for argument.

During the winter Captain Pike lost a number of his men from cold, starvation, and exposure in the vast Rockies. Late in February he, himself, crossed the Sangre de Cristos and camped in the San Luis Valley, where he was captured by the Spanish as an invader of their territory.

Pike had built a stockade on the Conejos River close to its confluence with the Rio Grande—a spot definitely not drained by the Mississippi and its tributaries and therefore outside the Louisiana Territory.

He said he thought he was on the headwaters of the Red River. Geographically his error was a matter of three hundred air-miles, since the source of the Red River is far across the Sangre de Cristo mountains in the Texas Panhandle. How he came to make this serious mistake has never been established.

Some historians contend that he was a young man totally ignorant of geography and that he was genuinely confused. Other historians hold that he was part of the Aaron Burr-James Wilkinson conspiracy to set up their own private little empire on the unknown and uncharted edges of the Louisiana Purchase. It is true that Pike's orders came from Wilkinson, Commanding General of the Army of the West, and not from the President or from Congress (as had the orders for the Lewis and Clark expedition). How much of a plot actually had been prepared by Burr and what Pike's part in this notorious scheme was are still moot points. In any case the plan of a new domain, if plan there was, came to an end with the conspirators' young agent in the hands of the Spanish, and high treason was never conclusively proved.

Pike was held a prisoner by the Spanish, first in Santa Fe and then in Chihuahua, until July, 1807, when he was released and reached Louisiana. After his return to the United States he devoted himself to writing an account of his journey. His book was published in 1810 and became an immediate best seller, both in English and in many translations. The "Grand Peak" or "Highest Peak" (as Pike described the mountain later to bear his name) and the land of Colorado became places of fascination to the whole world.

The result of Pike's expedition was to inspire quickening interest in Colorado throughout the East and Midwest. Intrepid trappers and traders pushed out into the wilderness to look for beaver in the high country and to trade with the Spaniards and Indians. These men were followed by official explorers and military officers heading parties. The next official explorer after Pike was Major Stephen H. Long, whose expedition in 1820 entered Colorado on a route up the South Platte. His party camped at several spots close to the Front Range and left by way of the Arkansas. Major Long thought the land was worthless and labeled eastern Colorado, on a map incorporated with his report, "The Great American Desert."

Later agricultural development, blooming lavishly along his exact route, was to make a liar out of Major Long. However, that time was a

18

half century later, when irrigation was developed and ditches were built to make the land flower. But in 1820 Long's report was believed and seriously retarded the region's settlement.

Yet simultaneously with eastern Colorado being deemed of no value, a romantic business, based on the feverish trapping of beaver, sprang up in the mountains. This was made possible because Mexico achieved independence from Spain in 1821, and a new era of friendliness was inaugurated with the United States. The whole Rocky Mountain region was thrown open to beaver-trapping, and trade was encouraged across the border. The actual boundary line between the two countries ran along the Arkansas River to the continental divide and then north to the forty-second parallel and so west. But the line was not taken seriously. The only serious consideration was beaver.

The gathering of pelts became immensely profitable because high hats for men came into vogue in all European and American cities. The hats were made from processed peltries of beaver which were found only in the mountains of Colorado and other western states. Many men set out from Canada and the eastern United States to provide the skins for fashion's dictates and the era of the trappers and the mountain men usurped the high country.

The period of the mountain men and the trapping of beaver was one of the most fascinating in the state's history. These trappers were the real pioneers of Colorado. It was they who braved the greatest dangers in this wild, unexplored country. In fact, two trappers arrived even before Captain Pike made his journey, and it was from the young explorer's pen that their activities became known. Pike met the two American men in New Mexico. Their names were James Purcell and Baptiste La Lande and, so far as we know, they were the first Americans to set foot on the land of Colorado.

Purcell, who left St. Louis in 1802, was one of a small group of adventurous men bound on a trapping and trading trip with the western Indians. The group spent three dangerous years on the plains of eastern Colorado, experiencing a series of terrifying escapes in Comanche, Kiowa, and Sioux raids. Eventually, in 1805, Purcell took refuge in the mountains where, before he came to Santa Fe, he discovered gold. This event occurred in South Park, an ample half century before gold excitement was to overwhelm the state.

La Lande, the other American, was sent out by an Illinois business house in 1804. He was supplied with beasts, laden with trade goods, which he was directed to lead up the Missouri and Platte River valleys and on to Santa Fe. He made the trip across Colorado without mishap

THE BEAVER CREATED A ROMANTIC BUSINESS

Trapping the beaver, shown above at work on his house, brought together mountain men, Indians, and Spanish or American traders for a yearly spirited rendezvous. Everyone had what was spoken of as a "fofar-raw" time (a corruption of fanfaron) while they transacted business.

and successfully sold the goods after he arrived in New Mexico. But instead of returning home with the profits, he married a Spanish woman and settled down in Santa Fe for the rest of his life.

These two men, Purcell and LaLande, were only the forerunners of many dauntless mountain men who started west in the early decades of the nineteenth century. Particularly after a commercial treaty between Mexico and the United States was signed in July, 1826, were the trappers drawn west. Some brought wagonloads of goods to Santa Fe for sale or trade, but most came to trap beaver in the high country.

Very few mountain men got rich. They became enamoured of the life and the land and never returned to civilization, although there were occasional exceptions. Such a one was General William Ashley, who organized a fur-gathering band called the Rocky Mountain Fur Company. He led his men west in the fall and winter of 1824-25. They entered Colorado by way of the South Platte, ascended the Cache la Poudre, made their way across the mountains, and camped on the Green River before fanning out for spring trapping.

Among his rugged young men were names that were to make Western history—Jim Bridger, Jim Beckwourth, Thomas Fitzpatrick, Louis Vasquez, and Jedediah Smith—all of whom led as dramatic and violent lives as the country they chose to explore. Probably the most famous mountain man in Colorado history was Kit Carson, who came later. He acted as guide and military officer in addition to his trapping activities. Many of these mountain men were unlettered; of those who could read and write, few chose to record their adventures. But luckily, as they opened up the country, adventurous travelers followed in their footsteps. The travelers described the life of those times so that the whole story is not lost.

One of these writers was young James Ohio Pattie, who came west in 1824. His account of the trapping days and the adventures the mountain men encountered graphically portrays life in Colorado during that era. In one place he tells of crossing the continental divide at a spot not far from Longs Peak in the winter of 1826-27 in these words:

"The passage occupied six days, during which we had to pass along compact drifts of snow higher than a man on horseback. The narrow path through these drifts is made by the frequent passing of the buffaloes, of which we found many dead bodies in the way. We had to pack cottonwood bark on the horses for their own eating, and the wood necessary to make fires for our cooking."

Such was the kind of crossing that the men of the Rocky Mountain Fur Company under Ashley had to accomplish before they could get to their destination.

General Ashley was not only unique in making money but he also chalked up a number of "firsts." He was the first to explore the northwestern corner of Colorado and to reach the Brown's Hole country, and. probably most memorable, he was the first manager to set up the custom of the *rendezvous*. Ashley chose a site on the Green River where all the band should return in July, bringing the skins they had obtained. This type of gathering became known as the summer *rendezvous* (to distinguish it from a lesser one in winter for sheltering purposes) and was a regular feature of the fur business for the next fifteen years. Having decided upon a place of meeting, the manager would bring in a quantity of supplies and goods. These were packed from the East by horse and mule train and later by ox-drawn wagons. The merchandise was available to his own men, independent trappers, or friendly Indians in exchange for skins and furs gathered during the winter.

For several days, while a whole year's business was transacted, celebrations and merriment were also in order. Horse races, gambling, drinking, dancing, story-telling, and swapping Indian wives were as much a part of the *rendezvous* as was the barter of beaver. Often the mountain men, who were an improvident carefree lot, would lose the result of a whole year's grueling work in the few days of a riotous *rendezvous*.

But not William Ashley. In a short three years' time, from 1824 to 1827, he made enough money to retire, a rich man. He sold out his Rocky Mountain Fur Company to a group of successors who carried on the business as long as there were beaver to be trapped and as long as the skins were in demand. Just about the time the beaver were decimated in the late 1830's, someone invented a top hat made of silk. All at once no one wanted beaver hats, only silk, and beaver became worthless in eastern markets.

The mountain men looked around for another occupation that would sustain them in the wilderness. The buffalo were roaming the plains of Colorado (as they had for centuries) and, with the beaver market fallen off, many turned their attention to the eastern part of the state and its buffalo. They began to shoot the big beasts and trade in their hides which were in demand as carriage robes, couch coverings, and the like.

Others had preceded them. Charles and William Bent and Ceran St. Vrain (builders of Bent's Fort on the Arkansas River) had been concentrating on this type of business since 1833. Lancaster Lupton, who came to Colorado in 1835 as one of the dragoons under Colonel Henry Dodge, had resigned his army career and built Fort Lupton on the Platte in 1836. Soon these forts were only two of a series scattered throughout the state, a couple even in the western section.

BENT'S FORT WAS A HAVEN

Built by the Bent brothers and Ceran St. Vrain in 1833, this huge adobe structure was the center until 1849 for the whole region's trade.

But, by far, the most famous and powerful was Bent's Fort built on the Arkansas halfway between the present towns of Las Animas and La Junta. It was the model for the rest. Constructed of large adobe bricks, it was oblong in shape, roughly one hundred eighty by one hundred thirty-five feet. The walls were fifteen-feet high and four-feet thick at the base. At two of the corners, the southwest and northeast, round bastions rose above the walls and projected out. Here were cannon and small holes for firing rifles. Entrance into the compound was made through a huge gateway where two heavy plank doors, plated with sheet iron, swung inward under a square watch tower. Around the interior courtyard were rooms, sheds, a warehouse, a corral, and complete equipment for withstanding a long siege.

In size and extent of influence it was like a small empire. The massive adobe structure that dominated the north bank of the river was only the headquarters of the business. Its contacts went hundreds of miles out in all directions. All the trade between Santa Fe and St. Louis passed this way, and one of the firm's partners was frequently in each city. The company's emissaries, particularly William Bent, who married a Cheyenne squaw, went down into Texas and up into Wyoming, gathering hides and trying to maintain peace with neighboring tribes.

Peace with the Indians and numerous buffalo hides were the keystone to a successful enterprise. As competition grew keener and the buffalo

SURE DEATH

The buffalo on foot was no match for a fleet Indian pony and the sure aim of a brave with sharp lance. Too short legs and great weight doomed him in the contest for his life.

herds were slaughtered with increasing wantonness, the plains tribes feared for the future. They needed to preserve the buffalo for themselves if the Indian way of life was to survive. Distrust of the whites, even such established, fairdealing traders as the Bents, increased.

Buffalo hides soon commanded a premium. To induce the Indians to bring them in, white traders met the situation by offering whiskey and firearms. Whiskey, known to have a demoralizing effect on any constitution, was even more violent with Indians. Its use produced an even quicker and more insane result than with whites. Addiction to alcohol among some of the Indians multiplied the violent episodes until there were cases when a whole band went berserk. The situation on the plains grew tense.

As incidents of treachery toward the white man mounted, the United States government established garrisons throughout the wilds and sent out military expeditions to impress the Indians. The first of these reached Colorado in the spring and summer of 1835, and was led by Colonel Henry Dodge in command of one hundred twenty galloping dragoons. His three companies entered by way of the Platte and left along the Arkansas.

The dragoons came again, ten years later, led this time by Colonel Stephen W. Kearny. He camped at the present sites of Denver and Pueblo, parleyed with the Indians, and shot off a rocket that zoomed toward heaven and burst on high. Terror struck the Indians since they thought the weapon was magic. But these expeditions produced no lasting results.

24

QUICK DRAW

After the Indians had been given firearms by unscrupulous traders, the fight between red man and white became increasingly s e r i o u s and required real speea in drawing to shoot.

The years of beaver trapping, buffalo trading and Indian skirmishes (that characterized the decades of Colorado history prior to the gold pioneers of 1858-'59) were also those of exploration. Certain celebrated explorers, such as Colonel John C. Fremont and Captain John W. Gunnison, made trips across the state. Colonel Fremont journeyed three times into or across Colorado in 1842, 1843, and 1845, sponsored by the United States Topographical Engineers, and again in 1848 and 1853, two trips sponsored by private interests. He employed such well-known guides as Thomas Fitzpatrick and Kit Carson, and on his 1843 trip was accompanied by William Gilpin. In later years Gilpin became Colorado's first territorial governor.

Fremont's first two trips explored the northern and western portions of the state. His third expedition concentrated on gathering data for military use in case of war with Mexico. At Bent's Fort on the Arkansas he detached thirty-three men under Lieutenant J. W. Abert, with instructions to explore the source of the Canadian River and to test this route as a military road to New Mexico. Fremont then continued up the Arkansas, past the highest peak in Colorado later named Mt. Elbert, over Tennessee Pass and on to the White and Green Rivers, and so to California.

Fremont's fourth trip was calamitous, and historians are still debating what went wrong. In 1848 railroad interests of St. Louis wanted to find a central route across the Rocky Mountains and offered to finance an expedition. An attempt to make the journey in winter was felt to be advisable since this would show up all the obstacles to be encountered

25

SPRING SNOW

Although it was some thirty years before railroads were built in the San Juans, snow conditions were accurately prophesied by the Fremont and Gunnison expeditions. These mountains offer a villainous terrain and the most dangerous slides in all Colorado. Conquering their grades and curves was an extraordinary feat of narrow-gauge engineering.

by future railroad builders. Fremont set out with thirty-four men and one hundred mules. He reached Bent's Fort in mid-November and, although trappers and Indians tried to dissuade him from his plan, he pushed on. After crossing the Wet Mountains and the Sangre de Cristos, he ignored the easy crossing of the continental divide at Cochetopa Pass and headed up the Rio Grande River into the heart of the perilous San Juans. Some say this decision was because of the poor advice of his guide, old Bill Williams; others contend it was due to Fremont's stubborn arrogance. Whatever the reason, the decision spelled defeat.

Disaster soon overtook the party. The deep snow, driving blizzards, and agonizing cold froze the mules where they stood. The animals toppled over dead. Bill Williams was sent to Taos for help on the day after Christmas. When no rescue arrived after sixteen days, Fremont himself took four men and started for New Mexico. With the aid of some Indians, relief for his party was finally obtained. But the final toll was the worst of any early exploration of Colorado. All the stock was lost and ten of the original thirty-four men were dead. Two more were lost when they went back for luggage left in the snows.

Fremont's fifth and last trip was with a private expedition in 1853 which crossed the state by way of Cochetopa Pass, a route just previously surveyed by Captain John Gunnison. This journey was uneventful.

In that same year of 1853 Gunnison had been employed to make a government railroad survey. He began his trip from St. Louis in June with eight engineers, a group of teamsters and employees, eighteen

26

SNOW TUNNEL

This photo and the one on the opposite page show different sections of the Silverton-Durango line. Each winter the D.&R.G. spent a vast sum of money in an effort to keep the branch open. At one spot a tunnel was encouraged to form from the snow itself. The brace may be seen over the two engines. At present the line operates only in summer.

wagons of supplies, and an escort of thirty mounted Riflemen. The party followed the Santa Fe Trail and its Mountain Branch across Colorado to the Huerfano River, a tributary of the Arkansas. They passed the beautiful Spanish Peaks, traced the Huerfano to its source, crossed the first range by way of Sangre de Cristo Pass and stopped at Fort Massachusetts near the western base of Mount Blanca, a year-old United States garrison used to quell Ute raids.

The Gunnison party explored the northern end of the San Luis Valley and decided on Cochetopa Pass as the most feasible route. They descended the Gunnison River (which they called the Grand) and followed the waterways to the site of Grand Junction. The party crossed into Utah, continuing their survey, and were at work on the Sevier River when Captain Gunnison and several of his party were killed by Indians on October 26. The survey was completed by one of Gunnison's lieutenants. The result of these two expeditions (Fremont's and Gunnison's) in 1853 was to prove the feasibility of crossing the continent, although not easily, by way of Colorado's high mountains.

During this exploration period, while Colorado was being investigated and mapped, the Mexican War broke out in 1846 and lasted for two years. Trouble had been brewing for some time between the United States and Mexico over questions of debts and boundaries; but annexation of Texas brought the trouble to a head. Colonel Stephen W. Kearny, later General, was chosen to head the "Army of the West." Volunteers were called for in May, 1846, and by June some sixteen

27

hundred men had been mustered in at Fort Leavenworth, Kansas. They marched to a camp on the Arkansas a few miles below Bent's Fort, on land later to be included in Colorado territory, and there made preparations for an attack on New Mexico and California. Bent's Fort itself was converted into a military storehouse and hospital.

Soon the Americans were on the march. General Kearny captured Santa Fe on August 18 after subduing only a token resistance on the part of the Mexicans. General Manuel Armijo, the crafty *commandante* in charge of their northern province, preferred politics to bloody war. After Armijo's surrender, Kearny set up a provisional government with Charles Bent at the head. (Charles Bent was the popular partner of Bent's Fort who resided in Taos.) Kearny left Colonel Sterling Price at Santa Fe in charge of the military, and marched on to California.

In the ensuing months distrust of the Americans under Bent and Price was fanned by the disaffected Mexican leaders who intrigued secretly in northern New Mexico. The result was a violent uprising against the Americans at Taos in January, 1847. Charles Bent was brutally murdered and scalped, despite the fact that he was married to a Spanish woman and had always been liked by the Mexicans. Many other Americans were slaughtered.

As soon as the news reached the United States military headquarters, Colonel Price marched north from Santa Fe and the revolt was successfully put down. Some one hundred fifty insurrectionists were killed or wounded. The principal Mexican leaders were captured, tried for treason, and hanged. The frightened trappers and traders who had fled to a refuge in Colorado returned home, and peace reigned once more in New Mexico.

The official ending of the Mexican War did not come until early in 1848 when the Treaty of Guadalupe Hidalgo was signed. The United States gained possession of the whole southwestern section of our present nation. In Colorado, all land south of the Arkansas River and west of its source was ceded to the United States by Mexico. Thus approximately two-thirds of the state changed hands, and Colorado became entirely American.

During the 1840's a number of travelers visited Colorado who left important records of the life in this region. Rufus B. Sage, later a Connecticut farmer, spent the greater part of the years from 1841 to 1844 traveling about the Rocky Mountain region in search of adventure and knowledge. When he returned home, he wrote an account of his travels, *Rocky Mountain Life,* in which he described nearly every portion of Colorado. His was an observant mind and his reminiscences of en-

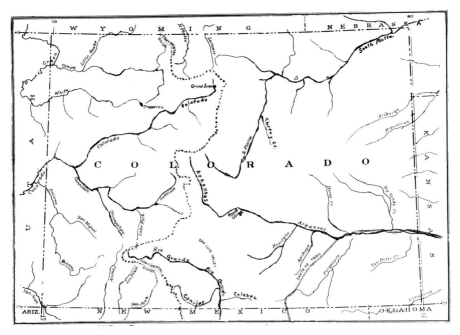

TRAVELERS FOLLOWED RIVERS, BATTLED MOUNTAINS

The main waterways are above. Below are the mountain ranges which are subdivided into many groups, too difficult to show in a small space. The Mummy, Never Summer and Rabbit Ears are to the north. Elk, Gore, Ten Mile, Mosquito, Collegiate, San Miguel, and Front are others.

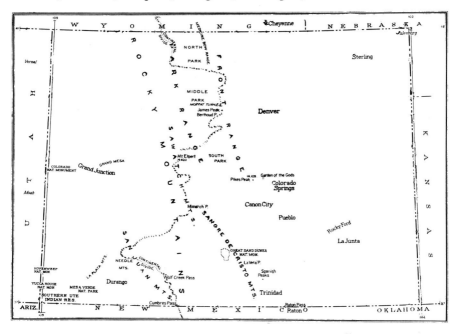

countering such interesting travelers as John C. Fremont, Baptiste Charbonneau, and Antoine Robidoux make good reading.

In the spring of 1846 Francis Parkman, a young historian, made the journey from St. Louis westward into Wyoming and Colorado which was later immortalized in his book *The Oregon Trail.* He traveled along the South Platte and left the state by way of the Arkansas, stopping at Bent's Fort for delightful entertainment within its stout adobe walls. Beginning in July of 1846 a young boy of seventeen, Lewis H. Garrard, spent nearly a year in Colorado with Ceran St. Vrain and William Bent, entering into the life of a trader with enthusiasm. He recorded his days of living in a Cheyenne tepee, eating dog meat and dancing with the Indians in the charming *Wah-To-Yah, and the Taos Trail.*

Leaving Taos in January, 1847, a young Englishman, George F. Ruxton, started his journey back to the United States by way of the San Luis Valley, the Sangre de Cristo Pass, Pueblo (where he visited a temporary Mormon settlement and also the trading post, Fort Pueblo), Fountain Creek, the Colorado Springs area, and South Park. Finally, early in May, he joined a wagon train at Fort Pueblo which was departing by way of the Arkansas River for "the States." His book, *Wild Life in the Rocky Mountains,* is indispensable for an understanding of Colorado during the 1840's decade.

But by 1850 the old days were dying. There was no more talk of beaver and buffalo. Now it was all about gold in California, settlers, and transcontinental railroads. In 1848 gold had been surprisingly discovered at Sutter's Mill in the Sacramento Valley. During the next year, while hordes of Easterners sought every means possible to bridge the three-thousand-mile gap between them and the sensational discovery in the Far West, in Colorado William Bent abandoned Bent's Fort. With the closing of this historic landmark after seventeen years of dominating much of the life in the state, an era came to an end.

During these years Colorado served mostly as a passageway or else was by-passed completely. Its mountains could be crossed by the most intrepid, but it was preferable to go south over Raton Pass and through New Mexico or north over South Pass in Wyoming. Both of these routes offered easier grades for long wagon trains and also smaller parties crossing the continent. A stream of settlers was moving westward, some to the gold of California, some to reach the new Mormon nation in Utah, and some to the loam of Oregon. A few stayed in Colorado briefly.

Notable among those who tarried in our region was the Mormon colony on the Arkansas at the site of Pueblo. In the winter of 1846-47 some two hundred seventy-five persons made up a one-street town there.

They built log shanties and a long temple of heavy timbers to use during the winter months. But when spring came, the Mormons continued on to Deseret. This was the name they had chosen for what they hoped would be an independent nation, free from American contact. Unhappily the next year, in 1848, all the Deseret land was ceded by Mexico to the United States and the Mormons found themselves in the same predicament that they had traveled a thousand miles to avoid. Utah was now American.

Colorado remained unpopulated until 1851 when the first permanent settlements did take hold. These were in the southern reaches of the San Luis Valley. As early as 1843 Mexicans had tried to found a town near the junction of the San Antonio and Conejos Rivers, northeast of the present town of Antonito. But the colonists were driven out by raiding Utes who resented encroachment on their hunting grounds. The defeated whites were determined to try again, and eight years later gained a solid foothold. The town of San Luis on the Culebra was started and was followed by San Pablo (then called San Pedro) in 1852 and San Acacio and Chama in 1853 at locations a few miles higher and lower on the Culebra. These four settlements on a tributary of the Rio Grande River in Costilla County have the honor of being the first towns in Colorado.

Their settlement was fostered by the government of Mexico and its land grant system. In an effort to promote towns on her frontiers, Mexico

FREMONT PASSED MOUNT PRINCETON

The Arkansas Valley, broad except for the Royal Gorge, is shown with Buena Vista nestling beside the waterway explored by Fremont in 1845.

OLD CHURCH

Our Lady of Guada-loupe was built in Conejos in 1858 and is the oldest church in Colorado. After this photo, some charming crudities were rectified.

made huge land grants to individuals who promised to plant settlers. Such individuals were also encouraged to develop the natural resources of Mexico's outlying territories. In this way title to thousands of acres in southern Colorado was given by Mexico to people for colonization. Later, when the treaty was signed between the United States and Mexico at the end of the Mexican war in 1848, the United States agreed to recognize the validity of the original land grants.

Among these grants were the Nolan Grant, immediately south of Pueblo, to Gervacio Nolan; the Vigil and St. Vrain Grant in the valley of the Purgatoire, to Cornelio Vigil and Ceran St. Vrain (one of the partners of the Bent's Fort enterprise); and in 1843 the Sangre de Cristo Grant of over a million acres, comprising Costilla County, Colorado, and a slice of northern New Mexico, to Stephen Luis Lee and Narciso Beaubien, a boy thirteen years old. Both grantees were killed a few years later in the Taos massacre of January, 1847, and Charles Beaubien, father of Narciso, inherited one half interest in the grant on his son's death and bought the other half from the estate of Luis Lee.

None of these grants succeeded in their purpose at the time of their inception because the Indians always proved too strong and drove the Mexicans back to more populous regions around Taos and Santa Fe. But in 1851 Charles Beaubien, owner of the Sangre de Cristo Grant, induced the colonists to try again. He recruited people from around Taos in sufficient numbers to stand off the Utes. After dwelling places were erected, he encouraged them to build irrigation ditches for their new farms, the first farms north of the present state line. In the decade of the 1850's more than forty irrigation ditches were constructed in this new region. These ditches have the earliest priority dates for water rights of any recorded in Colorado.

The first houses constructed were called *jacales*. They were made of logs set upright in a trench with the crevices chinked with mud. Adobe houses of a primitive type with sod roofs and earth floors soon fol-

FIRST FORT

Fort Massachusetts was sketched by a contemporary visitor as it nestled at the foot of Mount Blanca in a pretty situation that p r o v e d impractical.

lowed. These houses can still be seen in Spanish-American backwoods sections. Then, as now, the people raised chickens, pigs, burros, mules, goats, sheep, cattle, and horses, and tended crops of chile, potatoes, lentils, beans, wheat, and corn. Their little farms, ploughed with a crooked stick, were the forerunners of Colorado's lavish agricultural development.

The settlements were completely Spanish in character. Most of the inhabitants spoke no English and acknowledged only one religion— Catholic. Their folkways embraced numerous fiestas with singing, dancing, violin music, and guitar playing. They were ruled by an informal sort of government set up by the owner of the land grant. Civil authority was vested in a Judge of the Peace for each town; and religious authority in the priest of the district, who visited each village as often as he could make his rounds. These little settlements, although simple in structure, proved to be stable.

But in order to survive, the colonists had to have protection from the Utes. Consequently the United States established a garrison in 1852 at the foot of Mount Blanca called Fort Massachusetts. Disdainful of the small troop, the Indians were not intimidated by this gesture of protection and they continued to raid whenever they had a chance. A lone sheepherder was almost certain to be killed and his flock stolen to make a feast for the Indians. Sometimes they attacked the outlying farms, killed the workers and ran off the stock.

Finally their depredations culminated in a terrible tragedy at Fort Pueblo on Christmas Day, 1854. Chief Tierra Blanca and a band of his Mohuache Utes called at the fort with smiles and friendly gestures. Inside the fort seventeen white traders were celebrating the day with games and "Taos lightning" (the popular name for raw whiskey). In an expansive mood they invited the Utes to join them and swung open the gates. All went well at first until the contestants became embroiled in a fight over the winner. The Indians treacherously turned on their

33

GOLD PANNING

The arduous task of panning gold was practiced by all the early prospectors to test the streams or recover the gold that they were looking for. As they sloshed gravel around with water, the light material would be jostled out. But gold and iron (which were heaviest) would remain in.

hosts and murdered all the men but one. The single woman at the fort was made captive with her two children, and then the Indians went marauding off down the Arkansas, whooping for more booty.

The wounded man had been shot through the jaw and was unable to speak. He escaped to the Baca ranch, two miles below the fort, attempted to tell what had happened by signs and died a few hours later.

The government felt the time had come to take punitive measures. An expedition against the Utes was organized with Kit Carson of Taos as guide and a blistering campaign was conducted until the Indians sued for peace. As a result of this campaign Fort Massachusetts was closed. and in 1858 the garrison was moved to Fort Garland where a more advantageous location could be exploited to protect the few isolated settlers.

But mostly the vast state of Colorado was uninhabited in the early 1850's, at the time of the first efforts at colonization, with the exception of the original Indian inhabitants, the United States army garrison at Fort Massachusetts, and occasional die-hard trappers and traders such as those at Fort Pueblo. The majority of the adobe and log trading-posts were crumbling away. In 1853 when Captain Gunnison passed the site of Fort Uncompahgre or Robidoux Fort, built by Antoine Robidoux on the Gunnison River at the height of the beaver-trapping days, he found it already in ruins. A new wind was blowing in the high country.

That wind was the gold breeze. The rush to California had caught the imagination of the nation. In 1851 Horace Greeley, trenchant editor of the *New York Tribune*, published John Soule's article, "Go West, Young Man, Go West," and many followed their advice. When these young men arrived in California, only a minority were successful in finding gold, but many others caught the gold-fever.

At this period most of America's gold was still coming from the mountainous counties of northern Georgia, although these particular deposits were fast being exhausted. The Georgians were on the look-out for new fields, as were their brothers, the Cherokee Indians that had been displaced to the plains area. Many of them joined gold-seeking parties bound for California and traversed parts of Colorado, either going or coming.

One such party composed solely of Cherokees, who had mined in Georgia, went west in 1850. A good diary was kept of the trip by John L. Brown. (The Cherokees were an advanced tribe who used American names.) On June 21 the party left the Platte River and followed a creek up toward the mountains where a member named Lewis Ralston found gold. To commemorate the event the stream was named Ralston's Creek, and most of the party lay over for a couple days to investigate the gold deposits further. After concluding the deposits were not very rich, the party pushed on to California.

Ralston Creek still bears the name. It forms the Ralston Reservoir and flows by Arvada, Colorado. In 1857 it was the reason that another group planned a prospecting trip. William Green Russell of Georgia was married to a part-Cherokee woman who was a friend of Samuel Ralston. Ralston was a Cherokee Indian still living in Georgia and had heard about the gold-finding incident from his relatives in Indian Territory. Russell and his wife were interested by the episode.

Russell had not only mined gold in Georgia but also had made two gold-seeking trips to California, one accompanied by his brother, Levi J. Russell. The two Russells and a third brother, Oliver, determined to organize an expedition to Colorado. When they heard that the Cherokees in Indian Territory were assembling a group to return to Ralston Creek, the Russells opened correspondence with John Beck, a Cherokee preacher who had been a member of the 1850 party, and arranged to join forces with the Cherokees.

35

GREEN RUSSELL

William Greeneberry Russell, familiarly known as Green, was the greatest single cause of the Pikes Peak Rush which led to the founding of Auraria and Denver City and to the eventual growth of the state of Colorado. Had it not been for his courage and enterprise, it might have been some time before gold in adequately paying quantities was found to attract a western migration. Despite his having made money at first, he ended his years as a struggling farmer.

The Russells made up a party of nine residents of Lumpkin County, Georgia, and set out on February 17, 1858. Meanwhile Judge George Hicks, commander of the Cherokee party, had invited two Missouri companies of white men to accompany his band. Some difficulty ensued in getting the men and equipment for four parties ready at the same time, so the various groups proceeded westward at different paces. Eventually the Cherokee band and the Russell party, which had been increased to twenty-one, arrived at the junction of Cherry Creek and the Platte River late in June of 1858. On June 24 the Missouri companies overtook the other two at their camp in the cottonwood grove on the south side of Cherry Creek. This arrival of the two Missouri companies brought the number of men at the future site of West Denver to one hundred four.

The next day all four parties crossed the Platte and headed for their mutual destination, Ralston Creek. That night they camped on its banks. During the next days they prospected the Ralston Creek region and nearby territory. The men found a little gold, but were discouraged by the minuscule quantities.

Small crestfallen groups decided to return homeward across the plains. When signs of Arapaho and Cheyenne Indians on the warpath turned up, this movement was greatly accelerated. The Cherokees were a peaceful tribe and had no desire to be embroiled in a fight. On July 4 they announced they were going to turn back in a body. Most of the

WILLIAM N. BYERS

Probably no single man had as much to do with publicizing the two new little towns as the founder of the Rocky Mountain News who published his first issue, April 23, 1859. He was always a great booster and, for a time, had his office on an island in Cherry Creek between the two rival settlements. The flood of 1864 washed it away and made him decide on Denver as a permanent home. Byers was fearless in his campaigns for law and order in the new wild land.

whites were also rather cowardly and decided to accompany them.

Green Russell was not frightened and said that he was determined to stay if but two others would stay with him. When the decision was finally made only thirteen hardy men out of the one hundred four remained. These thirteen were either from Russell's original Georgia party or recruited by him on the way west. Russell and his men changed their camp to a spot close to West Dartmouth Avenue and Santa Fe Drive in present Englewood, Colorado, and there their tenacity of purpose was soon rewarded. On Little Dry Creek, which flows into the Platte, they found a placer. After the gold had been laboriously washed from the sand and gravel, it paid ten dollars per day per man.

These thirteen men worked on Little Dry Creek until the placer was exhausted. Then they spent the rest of the warm weather prospecting in the mountains, some of the party drifting as far north as Wyoming. Hostile Indians and a September snowstorm finally drove them south again. Much to their surprise when they returned to the cottonwood grove at the mouth of Cherry Creek on September 20, they found the place populated with new arrivals. Another party, a land-promotion company called the St. Charles, and several mountaineers and Indian traders, particularly Jack Smith and William McGaa with their squaws, had made camp there.

On September 6 the St. Charles Company had first staked out a settlement called Montana Diggings on the Platte, close to the Little Dry

UTE CHIEF

While the Plains Indians were c a u s i n g trouble, the Utes in the mountains w e r e at peace with white men. Later this was not so. In '87 Colorow, shown here, caused a small private war of his own.

Creek workings. Here they began to erect some log cabins. But a fortnight later they decided against this location. Then on September 24 they plotted the land on the north side of Cherry Creek's junction with the Platte, although the St. Charles group erected no buildings in their newer proposed town. They claimed they had a deed from the squaw men, John Smith and William McGaa.

The Russell party held a parley. They decided to establish a settlement in the cottonwood grove on the south side of the creek and, accordingly, acquired a similar title to the land from the Indian traders, John Smith and William McGaa. These titles were obviously dubious; but the traders contended that their squaw wives represented Indian ownership and were able to transfer possession. The Russells formed a town company and named the settlement after their home in Georgia, Auraria. The first log cabin erected in the new town was a double one, built by Green Russell and John Smith.

The St. Charles Company, meanwhile, frightened by impending winter, hurried back in October toward Lawrence, Kansas, their starting point. In Auraria Green Russell and his brother Oliver decided to lead a party of men "back to the States" to obtain more men and supplies for further prospecting the next summer. Levi Russell, secretary of the

ARAPAHO

Arapahoes and Cheyennes were tenants of most of Colorado's plains, and of the two, the Arapahoes were the more rebellious at the white man's encroachment. Here is a typical one in war bonnet.

Auraria Town Company, and a number of others planned to winter in the cottonwood grove. They busied themselves building cabins and getting materials from Fort Garland before the snows forced them indoors.

As the St. Charles Company wended their way eastward, they met numerous small parties of gold-seekers coming up the Platte. The news of Green Russell's find near Montana Diggings in July had spread swiftly throughout the Midwest, and even as far as New York. With each new telling, the amount of gold discovered increased until some of the wayfarers were anticipating untold riches as soon as they reached that vaguely defined land, the "Pikes Peak Region." In addition, a depression in 1857 had caused many farm mortgages to be foreclosed so that countless homeless farmers decided they might as well try gold mining as not. They joined the movement.

Alarmed at the numbers, the St. Charles Company dispatched Charles Nichols back to the mouth of Cherry Creek to hold their townsite. But one man was not enough. In the middle of November a group of brash town-promoters, led by William H. Larimer, arrived from Leavenworth, Kansas. The Larimer party decided to appropriate the St. Charles site. Charles Nichols protested. But the Larimer party notified him that a

LONE UNFORTUNATE WAGONS NEVER ARRIVED

The dangers of the long plains crossing to get to the gold fields were many and varied, especially for those parties that traveled alone.

"rope and noose" would be used on him if he made trouble. As a sop, they offered Nichols shares in their company, both for himself and his absent associates. Accordingly, on November 22 a constitution was adopted and officers were elected for the Denver City Company.

The Larimer group included three friends of James W. Denver, then governor of Kansas Territory. Before they had set off across the plains for the gold fields, these three men had asked Denver to appoint them probate judge, county supervisor, and sheriff of Arapahoe County. The governor, misled by the ballooning reports of mining activities on the South Platte, acquiesced, thus giving an official stamp to their real-estate junket. In return, the group called their new town Denver City, honoring Governor Denver.

During the first winter Auraria was the more important of the towns located at the junction of Cherry Creek with the Platte River. But each continued to grow astonishingly. By spring the new arrivals had turned into a swarm, and by summer, into a melee. In the middle of June Auraria had two hundred fifty cabins and Denver City, slightly more than half as many. But most of these were vacant. Everyone was away in the hills looking for gold. The "Pikes Peak or Bust" rush was at its height.

Substantial placer finds had been made in the spring of 1859 along a number of mountain creek-beds. Most notable was George A. Jackson's find in Clear Creek which was made in January of '59 at the site of

BETTER OUTFITTED EMIGRANTS SUCCEEDED

These wagons succeeded in arriving at their destination and camped on the west side of the Platte at Highlands (now called North Denver).

Idaho Springs, but was kept a secret until late April. This discovery was followed soon after, on May 6, by the finding of the first lode gold in Colorado. John H. Gregory, another Georgian, located the vein in Gregory Gulch, a tributary to the North Fork of Clear Creek. The spot is now within the limits of Central City. His find created the wildest excitement.

Late in May Green Russell returned to Colorado, leading a party of one hundred seventy men, and headed immediately for the mountains. On June 2 Russell found a fabuously rich placer in Russell Gulch, another tributary to the North Fork of Clear Creek. With these finds belief in Colorado's gold supply was definitely established in the minds of experienced miners despite the fact that the nation was still doubtful.

During March and April hundreds of hopeful tenderfeet, who were pulling into the little towns on the South Platte, had not known what to believe. They saw no gold and were beset by conflicting rumors. They spent their time deliberating on whether to return. Others turned back before they ever reached Auraria and Denver City. "Humbug" was shouted at the immigrants whom the "turn-backs" met on the trail, and the plains eastward were the scenes of strange confusion. Brash emigrants had started out to cross the six hundred miles, inadequately equipped and with the most meager knowledge of what lay ahead of them. Few gold-seekers had any idea of the distance they had to go. Some even attempted to walk the distance, pushing handcarts, and all

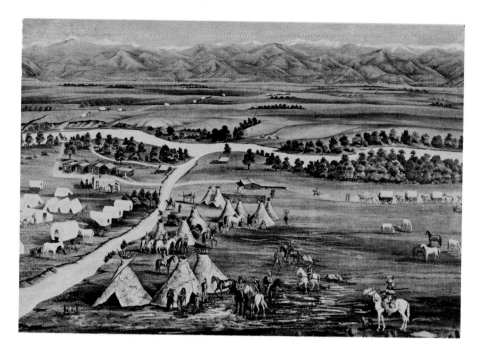

AURARIA AND DENVER WERE RIVAL TOWNS

On the south, or left, side of Cherry Creek, as it joins the Platte, can be seen the first row of cabins built in Auraria by the Russells.

encountered great hardships. Some were attacked by Indians and one starving, weakened party was reduced to cannibalism. Those that did arrive were downcast or angry when they found that the gold reports during the winter had been grossly exaggerated. At least half of those who actually completed the whole journey turned back after a few days' stay.

By May there was still a steady stream of canvas-covered wagons moving slowly westward across the Colorado plains along three main routes: the Arkansas, the Smoky Hill, and the South Platte. But an almost equal number were moving the other way. At Fort Kearny early in May nine hundred returning wagons passed in one week, and all offered to sell their outfits for almost nothing. Indignant signs were posted on the plains by bitter "go-backs" with messages such as

"Hang Byers and D. C. Oakes

For starting this damned Pikes Peak Hoax."

(William N. Byers and D. C. Oakes had both been loud in publicizing the gold rush or in offering guide books for emigrants.) Some of the wagons which had started out with hopeful signs tacked up: *Pikes Peak or Bust*, now carried new signs: *Busted by Gosh!*

42

An estimate of this rush and counter-rush has placed the number of gold-seekers who set out from the Missouri River during the entire spring of 1859 at 100,000. Probably 50,000 of these reached the end of their journey. And at least 25,000 of those who arrived at the Cherry Creek settlement were so discouraged that they returned home after a short stay. In April and May of 1859 there were spring blizzards in the Rockies and it was difficult for newcomers to verify the reports about Jackson and Gregory. But when the news was finally confirmed in June, the exodus east turned into a stampede in the other direction— toward the mountains.

By June 8 three reputable journalists had arrived from the East to inspect the Gregory Diggings. Together, they wrote a joint report. These men were Horace Greeley of the *New York Tribune*, A. D. Richardson of the *Boston Journal*, and Henry Villard of the *Cincinnati Commercial*. They emphatically verified the truth of the gold reports and gave exact amount and details of each mining company's work. John H. Gregory had already sold his discovery claim for $21,000. They were careful to warn amateurs of the dangers and labors involved in trying to dig gold from the earth, but few readers paid any attention to the warnings. They saw the word *gold* and not the word *hardship.*

FREIGHTING MADE DENVER FORGE AHEAD

By the end of 1860 the two towns merged. But the buildings on the north side of the creek multiplied faster due to closeness to roads.

FAIRPLAY

Fairplay, town of burros, was founded in 1859 by people who were dissatisfied with Tarryall, calling it Graball. On the edge, a restored town, now enclosed, called South Park City, has been designed for the museum-minded tourist.

The rush took on new momentum. Out on the plains covered wagons, that had turned homeward, now reversed themselves and set out for the gold fields once again with their occupants as gleeful as they had once been discouraged. Each day fresh emigrants left the outfitting places along the Missouri with signs on their wagons, "Pikes Peak or Bust." During the summer of 1859 a continuing flood of gold-seekers poured across the plains and on into the mountains to conquer the Front and Park Ranges. Such mining camps as Boulder, Gold Hill, Black Hawk, Central City, Idaho Springs, Georgetown, Dumont, Tarryall, Fairplay, Buckskin Joe, Breckenridge, French Gulch, and Negro Gulch sprang into being. In one month the population of the Gregory Gulch area jumped from fifteen to some ten thousand.

Settlements also were established at sites that would later develop into Pueblo, Colorado Springs, Golden, La Porte, Loveland, Trinidad, Canon City and the like. Regular stagecoach service was inaugurated to link these new towns with life in "the States," and freighting became a profitable business. A movement toward statehood for a new State of Jefferson was even begun because the Rocky Mountain settlements were so far away from the territories of which they were technically a part. But after a few meetings, the adherents to the idea of a Territory of Jefferson won. An appeal was made to Congress and officers and an organization were set up in an effort to achieve self-government. Although law and order were necessary, most of the population concentrated on mining.

44

BUCKSKIN JOE

Buckskin Joe, now gone, was named after its founder who dressed as a mountain man. This camp was the seat of the charming Silverheels legend. A prominent citizen in the '60's was H. A. W. Tabor, later a millionaire.

During the summer the experienced miners made fortunes. The sums they recovered from the gold fields do not appear very large today with the shrinkage of the dollar; but if multiplied by ten, the figures are more accurate. Both Gregory and Russell made $35,000 (about $350,-000 to us). Many others took out fortunes in gold—even a few lucky beginners. Since no figures were kept, it is impossible to know how many millions of dollars were supplied that year by the streams and mountains of the new gold-bearing region.

But for every tale of good fortune there was a counterpart. Many men were killed by Indians, burned to death by forest fires, drowned in the treacherous waters of the Platte, clawed to pieces by grizzly bears, died of gunshot wounds or exposure to the rigors of life in a high altitude, or became critically ill with the mysterious "mountain fever." The distinguished journalists had been all too correct in warning people to think carefully before setting out to look for gold.

When autumn came, many of the miners went back home across the plains to pass the winter. This group included the two discoverers, Russell and Gregory, who returned to Georgia. A very few stayed in the mountains. The rest chose to wait out the winter in the plains settlements, particularly Denver City, and this town gained population with sharp momentum. Regular theatrical productions, church services, and school attendance began in the autumn while a three-story business block, the largest yet, was erected at the corner of 16th and Blake Streets.

45

THE STAGECOACH BROUGHT WELCOME MAIL

The Pikes Peak Express began regular service in May, 1859, between Denver and "the States" and brought three journalists to tell of gold.

Consistently during the winter the settlement grew until in April, 1860, Denver City and Auraria decided to unite under the name Denver.

With its increased stability and population, the town was ready when a second gold rush rolled in during the spring months. But the 1860 rush was different. The incoming men came prepared and equipped, and most of them brought their families. The new arrivals, who numbered as high as 5,000 a week at the height of the season, planned to stay in Colorado and build homes in towns of their choice.

For the next decade the adjacent Gregory Gulch towns of Black Hawk, Mountain City, Central City, and Nevadaville were the most popular, and their combined population exceeded that of Denver. But Denver was the largest of the plains settlements. In large corrals, the most remembered being the Elephant Corral on Blake Street, gold from the mining camps was exchanged for supplies from the Midwest, and Denver remained the principal way station and freighting post.

The year 1861 brought two significant events to the new gold-regions —a formal government and the outbreak of the Civil War. During the two years since 1859, the self-styled Territory of Jefferson had been unable to function with any real backing, and problems of law and order had been settled by the local miners' courts, peoples' courts, and claim clubs, informal organizations set up by miners, townspeople, and farmers to record claims and boundaries and to perform rudimentary functions of policing.

Most of the settlements of the period were in either Kansas Territory, such as Denver, or in Nebraska Territory, such as Boulder. It was not feasible for the legislature of these two territories to exert authority across the wide and dangerous expanse of prairie which separated them from the new mining towns. Pioneers of the Pikes Peak region who had appealed to Congress for an independent Territory had been ignored.

But now Congress reconsidered. Considerable debate ensued on the proper name for the new territory with the result that the name of Jefferson was discarded in favor of Colorado. So named, the bill passed both houses, and on February 28, 1861, President James Buchanan signed the bill creating a Territory of Colorado with boundaries the same as those of today. It was left for President Abraham Lincoln to appoint the territorial officers.

William Gilpin was Lincoln's choice for governor. Gilpin arrived in Denver on May 27, 1861, six weeks after the firing on Fort Sumter. He stepped off the stagecoach to face not only the tremendous problems of a frontier region but also the added tensions of a nation at war with itself. Although Colorado's first gold development had been largely due to the initiative of the Southern Georgians, successive waves of immigration brought a preponderance of Northerners. A few minor riots occurred within the state's borders because of a division in sympathies, but Colorado was soon established as definitely Northern in sentiment.

Gilpin was an energetic man, a product of military training, and he set at his new tasks with vim. In fact his vim was so excessive that it later made him very unpopular, and he had to be replaced as governor. But it is due to his enterprise that Colorado achieved a spectacular military triumph in March, 1862.

The Southerners had conceived a brilliant tactical move. This was to send a force from Texas up the valley of the Rio Grande to try to

GAMBLERS AND FANCY LADIES ALSO CAME

Wells-Fargo took over the transcontinental Smoky Hill route in the mid 1860's and supplied transportation overland before the trains.

VIRGINIA DALE WAS A ROBBERS' ROOST

Highway men were another of the state's many problems in the Civil War period. Jack Slade, owner of this stage station, was a front man.

capture New Mexico and Colorado, thus shutting off the North's gold supply from California and from the new mines near Denver. If they could succeed in doing this, the Confederates then planned to march east through Kansas and surprise Grant in the rear.

Everything seemed to be going according to the Texan plan. The Rio Grande Valley, Albuquerque, and Santa Fe fell to them on schedule, and the Southerners were headed north. Then the Coloradans, recruited by Gilpin, made a forced march from Denver of nearly four hundred miles, covering a herculean ninety-two miles in the last thirty-six hours. Heroically they met the enemy at Apache Canyon, New Mexico, in a fierce and apparently losing battle; but through a clever circling maneuver by Major J. M. Chivington and his troops at La Glorieta Pass, the Confederate supply train was cut off. The battle was won, and the Texans were forced back to El Paso. The battle was proudly called "the Gettysburg of the West."

Unfortunately Gilpin had financed this campaign by issuing un-authorized drafts on the federal government. When local merchants found that they had sold mules, horses, and army supplies for a worth-less scrap of paper, the outcry against Gilpin necessitated his replace-ment. Eventually the federal government found a way to honor the drafts, but meanwhile John Evans arrived on May 17, 1862, as Colo-rado's second territorial governor.

John Evans was a prominent physician. He had been a personal friend and supporter of Lincoln and helped to found both Evanston, Illinois, and Northwestern University. After his appointment to the governorship of Colorado, Dr. Evans identified himself completely with the new territory and exerted a massive influence on its civic, railroad, banking, and industrial development.

Colorado was presented with several prickly problems during these years. Many of the settlers had returned to their homes in the East to enlist in the Civil War. The population fell markedly. In the moun-tains the miners had skimmed off the placer gold or surface "blossom rock" and had started to sink shafts. As the mines deepened, the veins yielded complex refractory ores whose reduction baffled everyone. On all sides the state was beset with poverty.

The Plains Indians chose this time to stage a final revolt against the white man's intrusion, deciding that the white enemy's many troubles made it an opportune moment to strike. In 1862, while the whites were preoccupied with the Civil War, the Indians began to

LARIMER WAS DENVER'S MAIN STREET

The freighting and stagecoach road up the Platte River entered Den-ver via Blake and Holladay (Market) Streets, fostering nearby growth.

PEACEMAKERS

Otto Mears and Chief Ouray were both remarkable men who did much for the state. Mears spoke the Ute language and was the Indians' friend. Ouray recognized the inevitability of the whites' dominance and co-operated quietly in signing peace treaties.

collect horses and firearms. They also tried to heal the longstanding enmity between the various tribes and thus to unite their own forces.

During the next two years a number of fruitless peace moves were attempted by the whites, but the situation grew increasingly worse. By 1864 Indian attacks along the stage and freighting roads were frequent, and ranchers were being murdered and scalped in surprise raids. The Indians planned a concerted attack on Colorado settlements for August 22, but a few friendly Indians revealed the secret. When the whites threw up defensive obstacles, the Indians realized their plan was known, and the attack was called off.

Governor Evans called a council of Indians in Denver in an endeavor to sign a peace treaty with Left Hand's band of Arapahoes and Black Kettle's Cheyennes. At first the older chiefs could not control the younger ones, and nothing was accomplished. Finally older and wiser heads in the tribal council prevailed. About the middle of October the Arapahoes came into Fort Lyon. (This had formerly been William Bent's new fort on the Arkansas which the government purchased in 1859.) Here the Indians handed over some of their plunder, and considered that they had complied with Governor Evans' terms of agreement.

After being fed for some days at the Fort, the commandant ordered them to camp at Sand Creek, where they were joined by the Cheyennes.

CHIEF'S WIFE

Chipeta was Ouray's squaw. Winsome and helpful, she endeared herself to many and is the heroine of several folk tales. She is buried outside Montrose where the Historical Society has erected a memorial and established a museum devoted to Ute Indian culture.

The two tribes formed a village of nearly seven hundred souls. They hoisted the American flag and a flag of truce in the center of their cluster of tepees and waited for the treaty-signing.

Colonel Chivington (the hero of the Battle of La Glorieta who had received a promotion) was heading a regiment called the "Hundred Days Men" which had been recruited to seek revenge on the Indians in the northern part of Colorado. This regiment had been patrolling the Platte River without any major Indian engagement because the wily red men kept out of the way. Frustrated, Chivington was in an impatient fury. The colonel decided to surprise the peaceful camp at Sand Creek (which was out of his territory) and slaughter the lot. His soldiers moved surreptitiously down the Arkansas, made their last march past Fort Lyon and out to the camp at night, and fell on the village at dawn.

The scene was indescribable as unarmed and friendly Indians were shot down in rows and their women and children slaughtered indiscriminately. Tents were burned, and horses and mules were captured. The colonel bragged in his report: "It may, perhaps, be unnecessary for me to state that I captured no prisoners." Throughout Colorado the name of Chivington became the center of acrimonious debate between those who defended his bloody action and those who condemned it. A Congressional investigation ensued and found that he had exceeded

FINALLY THE PLAINS INDIANS WERE COWED

The Plains Indians were camped at a spot about fourteen miles southeast of Sterling when they were attacked by U. S. troops on July 12, 1869.

his jurisdiction and "deliberately executed a foul and dastardly massacre." But to this day, such was Chivington's magnetic leadership, defenders are still writing historic pieces in an effort to whitewash his blackened name.

Instead of cowing the Indians, the Sand Creek slaughter only incited them to retaliation. Again the plains tribes went on the warpath, and Colorado settlers were thrown into panic. Raids were frequent. This unhappy condition continued throughout the next few years although, when the termination of the Civil War in the spring of 1865 released more soldiers for garrison and patrol duty, the Indian danger lessened.

The last two Indian battles on the Colorado plains occurred at Beecher Island in the Arickaree River in September, 1868, and at Summit Springs, some miles southeast of present Sterling, in the summer of 1869. In the former battle Chief Roman Nose was killed, and in the latter Chief Tall Bull went down along with fifty of his warriors. "Buffalo Bill" Cody acted as an army scout for this last engagement which terminated Colorado's troubles with the Plains Indians.

Colorado was preoccupied in the last years of the 1860's with a serious economic problem. This was the need for a railroad. The Union Pacific was engaged in constructing a transcontinental line which planned to by-pass Colorado. The state's mountains with their high passes were too formidable. The railway would touch only the north-east corner of the state and then move westward through Wyoming.

The future of Colorado and of Denver seemed doomed. Property values fell, as scores of families moved up to Cheyenne which, they believed, would be the coming metropolis in a more prosperous ter-ritory—Wyoming. But the less than four thousand citizens of Denver, although dismayed, did not despair. They organized a Board of Trade to build their own railroad and in one week in the autumn of 1867 raised $280,000 (later increased to $640,000 by the use of Arapahoe County bonds). With this money they organized the Denver Pacific Railroad and started grading a roadbed for a spur to meet the main line of the Union Pacific at Cheyenne.

The road was completed in June, 1870. Track was laid southward and the last spike was driven in Denver with a jubilant ceremony. The spike was made of solid silver, donated from the mines at George-town—a symbol of Colorado's wealth and her will to succeed. With the driving of that silver spike, the days of caroming stagecoaches, of breathless rides for the pony express, and of Indians on the warpath were ended. Colorado was free to expand.

The decade of the '70's achieved everything that the early gold-seekers had aimed for. It was a period of enormous growth and develop-

COLORADO NEEDED RAILROADS

Colorado's link with the nation was established in 1870 by two rail-roads. Then small lines like the D.S.P.&P. penetrated the mountains.

BUFFALO BILL

William F. Cody was a great showman who made the first step up the ladder of fame when he met a writer of dime novels, Ned Buntline, shortly after the Battle of Summit Springs when Cody had acted as scout for the cavalry. Later he developed a Wild West show and toured the U. S. and Europe. He is buried on Lookout Mountain, sixteen miles from Denver, a museum of his life relics nearby.

ment. The state's population tripled in five years. In 1870 it was 39,864, and five years later it was 120,000. Part of this influx was due to a second railroad, the Kansas and Pacific, whose roadbed came straight across the plains to Denver. The line was opened in August, 1870, just two months after the Denver Pacific puffed into the new union station.

That autumn a third railroad, the Denver and Rio Grande, was organized by William J. Palmer, and from then on its destiny was to be intertwined with the state's. It was a narrow-gauge line which, as the years went by, conquered deep canyons, high passes, and precipitous cliffs. Coloradans called it "The Little Giant." In 1871 it started building south from Denver. By the end of 1872 it had reached Pueblo and turned up the Arkansas to Florence.

The coming of railroads created new towns and also fostered the establishment of agricultural settlements called "colony towns." These towns were planned and organized in the East. The land was to be bought by community purchase and the work done on a co-operative basis. This form of settlement was well-suited to Colorado where irrigation projects required group planning. It also precluded the loneliness and dangers of individual and isolated ranches, and thus appealed to people in the East who wanted to move. Since the railroads had large tracts of land to sell, granted them by the federal government, they advertised extensively the "colony town" plan available for settlers. News-

THE UNSINKABLE

Mrs. J. J. Brown was an illiterate waitress in booming Leadville when she married. Her husband became a millionaire and she set out to conquer Denver society. Snubbed there, she moved on to Newport, and was successful. She achieved her greatest triumph as a heroine during the sinking of the Titanic when she acquired her sobriquet "The Unsinkable Mrs. Brown." Her life has often been dramatized.

papers throughout the nation publicized locations available under the attractive new scheme in Colorado.

The first of these towns to be organized was a German colony. It was promoted by Carl Wulsten, a Prussian editor of a Chicago newspaper, who wanted to ameliorate conditions of his fellow countrymen in the slums. In February, 1870, he brought three hundred men, women, and children with their household furniture, farm implements, and livestock by special train from Chicago to the end of the track and then by covered wagon to the Wet Mountain Valley. The town they founded was called Colfax after the vice-president of the United States. It was about seven miles south of Silver Cliff. But the co-operative plan was a failure. The members of the colony quarreled and broke up their holdings into individual lots. Others withdrew completely and moved away to nearby towns. Those who stayed farmed individually, and the town died.

The most famous of these "colony towns" was Greeley, named for Horace Greeley of the *New York Tribune* and organized by him and one of his staff, Nathan C. Meeker, through the columns of the powerful newspaper. The colonists began to arrive in April and May, 1870. They planted trees as soon as they had surveyed and laid out their town. They used a community lodging house and tents while they did their preliminary work. They built a community hall, a public school, bridges, ditches, and a fence enclosing the colony land all on a co-operative basis. Theirs was an idealistic group which centered their

55

"FACE UPON THE FLOOR"

In 1877 a New York author-actor, Hugh d'Arcy, picked up an artist who was drunk outside a saloon. This episode inspired d'Arcy to write a ballad with the above title. In 1936 Herndon Davis painted a face on the floor of the Teller House Bar which is a Central City tourist lure.

activities around their church and forbade the sale of liquor. The colony prospered and became the prototype for further enterprises of this kind.

Longmont, Evans, Green City, Platteville, Fort Collins, and Sterling all began in the next few years as "colony towns" or on a partially co-operative basis. Longmont erected fifty buildings in less than three months in 1871, so industrious were the town's four hundred colonists. Not all of this type of town succeeded (particularly Evans and Green City). But the wide publicity attendant on the forming of "colony towns" gave a great boost to agriculture throughout eastern Colorado.

In the mountains treatment of refractory ores was being solved, and mining prospered again. Professor Nathaniel P. Hill, a chemist and smelting specialist, erected a smelter at Black Hawk in 1868. By the early 1870's his smelter, the Boston and Colorado, was a success and was treating annually one to two million dollars worth of Gilpin County ores.

It was also during this period the Central City-Black Hawk area forged ahead as the cultural and society center of the state. Although Denver was making strides after the arrival of the two railroads, it had not caught up with the elite tone of the "Little Kingdom of Gilpin," as the new nickname was for the former "Richest Square Mile on Earth." In a snobbish sense the "best people" of the state were mostly residents of Gilpin County. Central City was far different from the ordinary run

OPERA HOUSE GEM

Central City's Opera House was built in 1878 by popular subscription for the citizens' own amateur performances. Later it fell into disuse and was abandoned to the mountain rats. Since 1932 it has housed an Opera and Play Festival that has brought world renown to the former gold camp.

of mining towns—amateur concerts and theatricals were of such a high standard that by 1878 the people were spontaneously impelled to build their own gem-like Opera House.

While Central City attracted distinguished Eastern travelers in the early 1870's and splurged by laying silver ingots in the street for President Ulysses S. Grant to walk on in 1873, other mining camps in the Front and Park Ranges and the Wet Mountains were equally prosperous. Silver began to be mined extensively in places like Georgetown and Rosita, and this metal enormously enhanced the state's economy. The southwestern part of the state broke into prominence in 1873 with discoveries of gold and silver, and the Utes were induced to give up their right to the San Juan Mountains in September of that year when the Brunot Treaty was signed. Summitville, Lake City, Silverton, and Ouray, spectacularly situated, were founded in the next two years as a new rush took place. Stupendous fortunes were soon being made against the background of the most precipitous peaks in the state, the rugged San Juans.

Not everything was cheerful in these years. In 1873 the East experienced a financial panic which had serious repercussions in Colorado. Eastern capital was withdrawn, railroad building came to a halt, and real estate values decreased. A dismal financial fog settled over the state, only to be followed by a worse disaster. The next two years were literally blackened by swarms of grasshoppers. They came in such

PLACERS GAVE WAY TO UNDERGROUND MINING

After loose surface gold was worked by sluice boxes and placering (as above), the deposits became exhausted, and mining required shafts, tunnels, drifts, and blasting in hard rocks to follow a vein. In the photo below, miners are drilling holes with double and single jacks.

SPECTACULAR SITES OF SILVERTON AND OURAY

Silverton was founded in 1874 and Ouray (below) in 1875. Both were the center of startlingly rich mineral belts which produced many enormous fortunes and led to years of extraordinary history. Today, Silverton's mines are gone, but the Camp Bird, Walsh's Ouray find, keeps on.

A DESERTER BUILT A GEORGETOWN HOTEL

Louis Dupuy was unique among Georgetown's colorful characters—a French chef, gourmet, and scholar. His pretty inn is now a museum.

clouds that they shut out the light from the sun. They settled like an ugly, wriggling carpet on the land, ate fields bare, and created such a depression that the federal government had to make an appropriation for feeding and clothing destitute farmers.

The question of statehood for Colorado had been bruited about for years—ever since the original discussion of a State of Jefferson in 1859. Advocates for statehood had made a series of efforts to win both the people of its region and the favor of Congress, but to no avail. Finally in 1876 the time was ripe, and Colorado was assured of being the thirty-eighth state of the United States when the citizens voted for the constitution submitted on July 1. Most Colorado towns celebrated three days later, on the Fourth of July.

In Denver a colorful parade was staged followed by a patriotic program in the cottonwood grove beside the Platte. Among the many floats was a "Grand Car of the Union." This consisted of two flat wagons joined together and pulled by six white horses. Thirteen women rode on the first wagon, dressed in costumes representing the original colonies. On the rear wagon thirty-seven girls representing the thirty-seven states of the union were grouped about a seat of honor where pretty Miss Colorado posed as the new thirty-eighth state. She was charming Mary Butler (later Brown) and in 1951 she was still alive to take part in the state's seventy-fifth birthday.

A CANNIBAL ATE DEMOCRATS IN LAKE CITY

Legend says Alferd Packer was sentenced to be hung because he "et up five of only six Dimocrats in Hinsdale County." The truth is grisly.

Since its enabling act was passed just one hundred years after the founding of the nation, Colorado was called the "Centennial State." President Ulysses S. Grant affixed his signature on August 1, 1876, which led to the custom of celebrating August 1 as Colorado Day.

Governor John L. Routt, who had been the last territorial governor, was elected the first state governor. He was well equipped to get the new state's political machinery in motion. The first state legislature convened in November and chose Henry M. Teller and Jerome B. Chaffee to serve as Colorado's first United States senators, while James B. Belford had the honor of being the state's first congressman. All these men had started their Colorado careers in Central City, and, as time went on, an increasing amount of political power was to fall into the adept hands of the men from the "Little Kingdom of Gilpin."

During the next couple of years Colorado continued to concentrate on its two main activities, mining and agriculture. But another business began to be of increasing importance. When more and more mines were opened, perched high on inaccessible mountains, the problem of transporting the ore out and supplies in became a major one. Packing and wagon-freighting grew into a business that employed thousands of men and animals. The crews reached perilous heights along slim ledges before the narrow-gauge made its way into the mountains. Even

TOLL ROADS

Otto Mears built over four hundred and fifty miles of toll roads in the San Juans in crder to solve the transportation problem. He was given the nickname of "Path- finder of the San Juans." This is typical of his road structure, a stretch near Ouray still in use.

after the narrow-gauge's arrival the crews continued their hauling as feeders to the railway lines.

Toll roads were started to take care of this freighting business. The most spectacular toll roads were built by Otto Mears in the jagged San Juans. This little man was one of the great pioneers of the state. His pack trains, toll roads, freighting outfits and his four little narrow-gauge railroads interlaced the dramatic peaks of southwestern Colorado with a tracery of perilous transportation routes. Today his railroads are gone. But many of his roadbeds for wagons and rails are in use for oiled highways, the most noted of which is the Silverton-Ouray road, the scenic "Million Dollar Highway."

The decade of the 1870's closed with a series of striking events. The first was the discovery of rich carbonates of lead and silver ore in the mountains close by Leadville. The rush to the district began in the summer of 1877 and continued full blast for two years. The town's population jumped from less than a hundred in Oro City to almost 30,000 in adjacent Leadville in just a few years.

Millionaires were created over night. The most talked-of rise was that of Horace A. W. Tabor, general storekeeper, who in the spring of 1878 grubstaked two prospectors to seventeen dollars worth of supplies, followed by a second hand-out, bringing the total to about sixty-four dollars. What his partners, August Rische and George Hook, found was the Little Pittsburgh mine, a bonanza whose silver ore ran $200 a ton. Tabor began investing in other mines and by the end of the year

FREIGHTING

Getting supplies into the mines and ore out was big business, and profitable to boot. A number of early fortunes had their foundation in the work of lowly oxen and mules and the supplies they hauled. This 1879 view is of a wagon train crossing Ute Pass.

his holdings were incorporated in a twenty-million-dollar company. He was now Colorado's "Silver King" and moved up that autumn from his office as mayor of Leadville to lieutenant-governor of the state.

Leadville was nicknamed the "Cloud City" because its altitude is 10,200 feet, nearly two miles above sea level. It saw the beginning of many big corporations besides mining companies such as Tabor's. The May Company Department Stores started in a tent on Harrison Avenue, operated by David May. The American Smelting and Refining Company, owned by the Guggenheims, opened its first smelter there. The wildness and excitement of Leadville's boom made all other Colorado rushes pale in comparison, while the richness of its ore hit fantastic new figures. In a single day, for example, $118,500 was shipped from the Robert E. Lee mine on Fryer Hill.

At the height of the boom accommodations were at such a premium that hotel keepers in log structures rented out beds in shifts of eight hours each. Other arrivals counted themselves lucky to be able to sleep on the floor of a boarding-house tent. Every trail was used that led to Leadville—up the Arkansas, up the Platte and over Mosquito Pass and Range, up Ten Mile Creek and over Fremont Pass—any route would do as people poured into town via stagecoaches, wagons, horseback, and even on foot.

Carlyle Channing Davis, later to publish the *Leadville Chronicle* and still later to record his reminiscences in a book, *Olden Times in Colorado,* has left us a good picture of his impressions when he arrived in January, 1879:

THE RICHES-TO-RAGS STORY OF BABY DOE TABOR

Above is a window of the second Mrs. Tabor's glamorous life when she married the Silver King in a $7,000 wedding gown in Washington.

"The scene unfolded was unlike anything I ever before had seen or conjured in my imagination. The main thoroughfare (Chestnut street along California Gulch—C.B.) was pretty closely and compactly lined with houses on either side, for a distance of two miles, following the contour of the gulch, all of log or rough-hewn slab construction, only a few of them two stories in height. Every other door seemed to open upon a saloon, dancehall or gambling den. There were no street lights, but the thousands of coal oil lamps indoors cast fitful flashes of baneful light across the way.

"The boardwalks on either side were filled to the center with a constantly moving mass of humanity, from every quarter of the globe, and from every walk of life. The stalwart teamster jostled the banker from Chicago. The deep-lunged miner, fresh from underground workings, divided the walk with debonair salesmen from Boston. The gambler and bunco-steerer walked arm in arm with his freshest victim picked up in the hotel lobby . . . .

"At that hour, long past midnight, few could have had any other mission than sight-seeing, hence the mass was constantly being augmented

COLORADO'S MOST POPULAR LEGEND

The former beauty spent days tramping the streets of Denver seeking aid in an effort to follow Tabor's wish: "Hang on to the Matchless."

or diminished by the crowds pouring in and out of scores of resorts with which the thoroughfare was lined . . . .

"Belated Concord stages, hauled by six-horse teams, huge freight vans, lumbering prairie schooners, and all manner of wheeled vehicles, were toiling up and down the street, separated from the boardwalk by parallel lines of snow, piled in the gutter to a height of three or four feet . . . .

"Taking in the spectacle, I joined the throng, passing from door to door and witnessing scenes that almost beggar description. Chief among the places I visited was Pap Wyman's combination concert and dance hall, with every game of chance known to the fraternity in full blast— faro, keno, roulette, stud poker, pinochle and what not. On the face of a monster clock, behind a bar scintillating with a wealth of crystal, was painted the significant invitation to guests 'Please Do Not Swear.'

"Here, perhaps, were a score of girls and women of the underworld, of varying ages and types of attractiveness. They were attired in more or less picturesque and fantastic garb, some wearing little surplus apparel of any description, and were dancing with bearded bull-whackers, un-

EARLY LEADVILLE WAS THE REAL THING

*A view of Harrison Avenue, looking north at the height of the boom
in 1878. Five excellent summer museums now recreate this lively time.*

couth delvers in the mines (with soil besmeared attire to mark their
vocation), with the dapper clerk out for a night's lark—with anybody
and everybody disposed to clasp their soiled waists, whirl them through
the mazes of a two-step or a polka, and then accompany them to the
bar . . . ."

Davis stayed up until dawn. At three in the morning he attended a
vaudeville performance and watched the miners throw silver dollars in
showers at the feet of the actors and actresses who made a hit. When
the sun was lighting up the snow peaks of the Sawatch and Mosquito
Ranges, he returned to the Grand Hotel. There, he found his sleeping
partner gone "and a warm although not wholesome bed awaiting." He
was soon asleep and dreaming of the fortunes to be made in this lusty
town.

To reach Leadville's bonanza ore both the Denver and Rio Grande
and the Santa Fe railroads started hastily laying track up the Arkansas
River. The Royal Gorge between Canon City and Salida was too narrow for more than one track to pass through. As fast as the crew of
one company laid rails, the men of the other company tore them up.
The brawls and fights over possession of the Royal Gorge caused the
contest to be carried to the Supreme Court. Here, is was decided that
the prize Gorge would be awarded to the Denver and Rio Grande;

MODERN BUCKSKIN JOE IS A RESTORATION

*Not far from Canon City in conjunction with its Royal Gorge develop-
ment, an 1860 town may be seen. Note false presence of women here.*

but that this railroad would forfeit to the Santa Fe any right to lay track
south of the state boundary. That territory would be reserved for its
rival. Happy at the outcome, the Denver and Rio Grande hastily began
laying track again and reached Leadville in July, 1880.

While this brawling trouble was going on, another bitter problem
confronted the state. For fifteen years, under the wise and pacific leadership of Chief Ouray of the Southern Utes, the whole tribe had been
friendly to the white man and had given way without outward rebel-
lion to encroachment on the Ute hunting grounds. As the greed of the
white man continued to mount and the hunting became poorer and
more restricted, the Utes grew restive. The younger chiefs, especially
those of the Northern Utes, were inclined to rebel against Ouray's
counsel and the peaceful stand of the Southern Utes.

This situation was aggravated by the placing of Nathan C. Meeker
in the White River Indian agency. Meeker had made a success of founding the "colony town" of Greeley and starting its agriculture. He became imbued with the idea of attracting the Utes away from hunting
to farming, and sought the position of Indian agent. Unfortunately he
was ill-equipped by nature or training to deal with Ute psychology.
His "do-good" attitude antagonized them, and when he ploughed up
the track where they raced their ponies, their menacing gestures frightened him.

DOC HOLLIDAY

Glenwood Springs has erected a fine marker on the former gunman's grave which adds, "He died in bed," an ironic twist to the gambler's life. He operated in Pueblo, Denver, and Leadville but led a quiet career at the famed hot springs spa where he died in 1887.

Meeker sent for military aid, and Major T. T. Thornburgh was dispatched from Fort Steele in Wyoming to move south with a troop of one hundred eighty men. That was the signal for the firebrand younger chiefs to arouse the Northern Utes. They attacked the agency, killed eleven men, including Meeker, and captured three women and children. While they were burning and pillaging the agency, another band of Northern Utes ambushed Major Thornburgh in Milk Creek. The major and thirteen of his men were killed.

The remaining soldiers corralled the train and made a breastwork of dead horses, wagons, and supplies to withstand a siege. The Indians were on higher ground, concealed behind rocks and trees, and shooting constantly. That night Joe Rankin, the scout, stole away to ride for help. He covered one hundred sixty miles in twenty-eight hours to reach Rawlins, Wyoming. As a result, relief from General Wesley Merrill's command reached Milk Creek on the sixth day of the battle. The Indians scattered, and a man with a white flag rode forward from their group. He was a runner from Chief Ouray of the Southern Utes who had been sent north to order the fighting stopped.

Reprisals on the part of the military were forbidden by Washington. After an investigation, it was decided to move the Northern Utes into Utah and to confine the Southern Utes to a fifteen-mile strip in southwestern Colorado. In September, 1880, the Utes were forced to evacuate to the Uintah agency in Utah. Happily, Chief Ouray died in August and did not have to live to see this disgrace meted out to his people. Although compensation for their lands had been promised the Utes, no effort was made to pay this money until seventy-five years later when the tribe finally won a Supreme Court decision.

Simultaneous with the settling of the Ute trouble in Western Colorado

BAT MASTERSON

Denver police ran Bat out of Colorado in 1900 as a dangerous drunk. He had lived there and in Creede for eleven years and married in Denver in 1891. He was a gambler, bartender, theatrical manager and a sports promoter. He died in New York, 1921.

and the excitement caused by the Leadville boom, mining zoomed throughout western Colorado. A series of new camps sprang into being in the late 1870's and early 1880's. Notable among these was Silver Cliff in the Wet Mountains which was founded in 1878 and by 1880 was rated the third largest city in the State. (In the 1950's its population had fallen to around two hundred.) Others that boomed at this period were Aspen and Ashcroft in the Elk Mountains (where silver discoveries were made in 1879); St. Elmo up Chalk Creek in the Collegiate Range of the Sawatch Mountains; Pitkin, Ohio City, and Tin Cup on the western side of the Sawatch Mountains; Crested Butte, Schofield, Gothic, and Irwin in the southern Elk Mountains; Red Cliff in the Gore Range; Bonanza in the Cochetopa Hills; Telluride, Ophir, Rico, and Placerville in the San Miguel Range of the San Juan Mountains; Lulu City and Teller in the Never Summer Range, and many, many more.

Most of these new strikes were silver ore but some were gold and some a gold-silver mixture. By 1879 most of the population of Colorado had been on the move for twenty years, constantly chasing the pot of gold at the end of the rainbow—which was always over the farthest mountain in the next canyon! And more often than not, it actually was.

The life of the miner, like the life of the trapper in the mountain-men era, was hard work. But it carried much of the same buoyancy with it and in the case of the miner there was always the hope of striking it rich. The prospector, like the trapper, set off alone into the wilderness, carrying all that he possessed with him. In the prospector's case, he had the burden of grub, a gold pan, specimen pick, shovel and ax instead of traps, and often he was accompanied by a faithful burro. But the

THE MATCHLESS MINE IS THE BEST KNOWN

The Matchless mine was a bonanza that poured forth silver worth as high as $100,000 a month, shown in 1935 after Baby Doe was frozen.

distances and tortuous terrain that each covered were alike staggering feats. Although many miners did carry some staples for eating, both sets of men depended mostly on venison for food and had to be brave hunters as well.

The early prospectors tested each stream by "panning" gravel to see if, when they sloshed the water and gravel around and out of the pan, there would be any traces of glittering color left in the bottom. If there was color, this was sure to be gold. Then the prospector had to search for the exact placer bar or vein of ore that was producing the color in his pan and stake out a claim in the richest spot. Mysteriously the news of his find always traveled swiftly through the wilderness, and others started mining in the new ground.

The first placer claims were worked by very primitive methods. After panning established the fact that gold was to be recovered, some of the miners built "cradles" or "rockers" where pans and screen were placed on barrel staves and rolled back and forth with a stick as a handle. Others constructed "long toms" for the same purpose. If the placer claim proved rich, the men built a sluice box which resembled a descending flume with riffle boards and cross bars at intervals along the bottom. Quicksilver was placed behind the cross bars to catch the heavy gold which sank to the bottom each time pay-dirt was shoveled into the box and washed down the sluice. Water ran from a ditch into the sluice or was bucketed in from a dammed pool. Soon a creek would contain a whole series of small groups of men busily sluicing gold.

As soon as a good strike was made, a rush followed. All the "boomers" hurried to stake claims and to found a town, throwing up log cabins and board buildings with false fronts. If the strike proved profitable enough to move into the second phase of hard-rock mining (where shafts and tunnels were dug and ore was blasted from continuing rich veins), the town took root. Otherwise the camp might have a population of two or three thousand for a couple of years, or until the placers and small veins were exhausted, and then everyone moved out. leaving the town deserted. Sometimes news of a recent strike was so entrancing, that people departed in a scrambled hurry. Heedless, they left everything behind, furniture in the cabins and dishes on the table, as they stampeded to get to the new strike.

Many of the towns founded in the earliest 1859 rush, such as Tarryall in South Park and French Creek on the Blue River, were already ghost towns by 1879, and many more of those that started in the late 1870's and early 1880's were to have only short lives. Today Colorado is dotted with mining ghost towns that in 1879 were booming hamlets (and often grandiosely called "cities" in the fashion of the times) that were supported by rich mines, now completely worked-out.

The year 1879 may have been one of Indian conflict and of mining excitement in the mountains, but in Denver a delightful invention was installed that had people engaged in friendly, exclaiming conversation. This was the telephone. Frederick O. Vaile secured one hundred sixty-one subscribers for a proposed system and in February installed a switchboard at 1514 Larimer Street. The mechanism was far from efficient but the idea caught on. The "talking-wire" delighted everyone.

A few months later the "Silver King," Horace Tabor, installed a system in Leadville. Soon Golden, Central City, Black Hawk, Georgetown, Boulder, Colorado Springs, Pueblo, and Gunnison had operating systems and by the end of 1879 a long distance, or toll line, the wonder of the age, ran from Denver to Georgetown and from Denver to Leadville. The latter line was under the sponsorship of Lieutenant Governor Tabor who spoke from Leadville to Denver on December 14. According to the *Leadville Herald*, Tabor heard the voice at the other end of the wire as easily as if the person were talking on the Leadville exchange.

"What won't science think of next?" the editor asked.

About this same time cattle ranches had taken over the vast plains in eastern Colorado, formerly tenanted by buffaloes and Indians, and here the picturesque life of the open range was in full swing. In 1877 John W. Iliff, one of the great cattle kings who began raising cattle in

71

the 1860's, had expanded his holdings of water holes along the South Platte until he was running a herd of some 35,000 head. He actually owned about fifteen thousand acres but controlled many thousand more acres by holding "frontage" along the river. He imported thousands of Texas longhorns each year as well as thoroughbred shorthorns in order to improve the blood of his own herds. During the summer seasons he employed forty cowboys with two hundred horses to manage his drives and roundups. The prairies which had been a sea of massive dark brown humps while the buffaloes grazed now flashed with the tossing of five-and-six foot spans of white longhorns.

The romantic life of the cowboy (to be glorified for decades afterward in pulp magazines and on the screen) dominated nearly half the state. In the succeeding years many other large cattle companies were formed, a number directed from Great Britain. The Prairie Cattle Company, backed by British capital, ran more than 50,000 head of stock and controlled more than two million acres of Colorado's plains land. Roundup of cattle and branding of calves took place on a stupendous scale.

The roundup, a unique feature of the cattle industry, is still held today but with much smaller herds. All the owners or managers running cattle on the range of a given district, would gather at a good camping spot and bring along cowboys enough to handle the cattle they owned. Each ranch had a foreman in charge of its cowboys and these in turn elected a foreman who directed the one or two hundred cowboys assembled.

In the South Platte area the camping ground was near Julesburg, and from there the cowboys and foremen would fan out over the plains, rounding up the cattle, castrating a majority of the young bulls, and searing a mark on each calf with the same brand as its mother's. Moving up the valley at the rate of five or ten miles a day and making camp each night, the band of riders slowly inspected and separated all the cattle for hundreds of miles around. When the whole troop was in motion, it created a great spectacle with its many chuck wagons, hundreds of horses, and thousands of cattle kicking up an enveloping curtain of swirling dust. Similar roundups were held, moving up the Arkansas and Arickaree Rivers from the eastern edge of Colorado, and still other roundups on a smaller scale were held annually in various sections of the state. In the autumn the cattle were gathered again in a different sort of roundup in order to weed out the animals ready for shipping to market.

These enormous cattle ranches lasted only a short time. As population increased "nesters" came in. Feuding between the two interests re-

BOULDER'S UNIQUE SPOT FOR A CAMPUS

*The first classes at the University of Colorado began in September,
1877. Attendance and buildings expanded fast during the next decades.*

sulted. Many are the stories of theft, arson, and murder which date
from those violent days when the cattlemen tried to intimidate the home-
steaders. During their swashbuckling reign they increasingly over-
grazed the land and diminished their own profits. In addition the demand for agricultural produce began to exceed the demand for meat,
and in 1887 a crippling cold winter with excessively heavy snows killed
off great herds of stock. Finally the cattle companies had to recognize
an inevitable trend. After only two decades of existence, the enormous
ranches of the Colorado plains were broken up.

But this was one of the few aspects of life in Colorado that waned
during the booming 1880's. Nearly every other phase was thriving; no
decade of the nineteenth century in Colorado history was more prosperous. The state's story narrows itself down to a recital of new place
names and mounting figures. Principal factor in this expansion was
railroad trackage. Old roads built new routes into every corner of the
state, and new roads entered its borders.

The new railways that moved in from the East were the Burlington,
Rock Island, and Missouri Pacific. The Union Pacific added its Julesburg cut-off up the valley of the South Platte in 1882. The Kansas
Pacific and the Santa Fe (both of which had arrived in the 1870's)
brought the total of railroads that entered the state to six. These main
arteries pumped life blood across the plains into the economic system
of Colorado and produced a fine glow of health.

TEAPOT

Pictured at Montrose, a narrow-gauge engine snuggled alongside a broad-gauge steamer. It was called a teapot or sewing machine.

The Denver and Rio Grande, the Colorado Central, and the Denver South Park and Pacific extended their narrow-gauge tracks in every direction, conquering passes and executing prodigious engineering feats. One of the most remarkable of these was the Georgetown Loop, completed by the Colorado Central in 1884 in order to reach Silver Plume. Another feat was the conquering of the Black Canyon of the Gunnison by the Denver and Rio Grande.

The Colorado Midland, a standard-gauge line, began building from Colorado Springs over Ute Pass and Trout Creek Pass to Leadville in 1885. From there it gained the western slope of the Sawatch Mountains through a tunnel under Hagerman Pass and raced down the Frying Pan in an effort to reach the richness of Aspen's silver ore before the Denver and Rio Grande could get to the booming new camp. At Basalt it turned up the Roaring Fork but did not arrive in Aspen until February 4, 1888. This was because the Midland ran into difficulty in building high, long bridges over Maroon and Castle Creeks just outside the city limits.

The Denver and Rio Grande had already reached the "Silver Queen" (as Aspen was nicknamed) on November 1, 1887. Its route was by way of Tennessee Pass and the valley of the Colorado River to Glenwood Springs where it, too, turned up the Roaring Fork. The exuberant camp of Aspen staged a gala reception to welcome the "Little Giant" when the narrow-gauge line arrived. Dynamite was shot off and a torchlight parade held. For mountain towns like Aspen, railroads meant the end of desolate isolation and an opportunity to move ore out to the smelters and to get supplies in. Such traffic spelled prosperity for the railroads, too, and by the close of the decade the trackage laid in Colorado had leaped from 1,570 miles in 1880 to 4,176 miles in 1890.

Mining in the mountains continued to flourish in the late 1880's and early 1890's. and occasional new camps sprang up. Aspen and its theatri-

FULL STEAM

This photo shows a heavy train pulling into Craig, a section of line now belonging to the D.&R.G. but formerly to the Moffat Road.

cally rich ore were the sensation of this period, although its boom never took on the wildness of the Leadville rush. Aspen attracted a more substantial type, people such as the New York financier, Jerome B. Wheeler, who built the Wheeler Opera House and the Jerome Hotel. At the same time the camp's isolation precluded a very fast growth and made it less enticing to the underworld element and the confidence men. It had one block of parlor houses and red light district, known as "the Row," but its gambling dens and variety hall never held a candle to the many in Leadville.

The richness of Aspen's silver ore surpassed that of any other Colorado camp. Its Mollie Gibson and Smuggler mines produced tonnage that in some instances was almost flawless metal. Fantastic nuggets were hoisted up their shafts, and during the next decade the Smuggler mined the largest silver nugget ever found. It weighed over a ton before being trimmed. During the late 1880's, after the town acquired a smelter and railroads, Aspen's silver production ran around six million dollars yearly. It mounted until 1892 when, with a production of $7,080,538, it surpassed Leadville's output of slightly more than five million dollars for the same year.

Leadville in Lake County, Aspen's greatest silver rival, began its existence in 1879 and 1880 with an annual mineral production of around fifteen million dollars. By 1890 this was reduced to roughly eight million dollars, a figure which declined each year. The earlier mining camps in Gilpin County and Clear Creek County, such as Central City and Georgetown, continued to hold their own, and each county produced around two million dollars yearly. Throughout the state silver production far out-distanced gold during the 1880's, and the over-all figures ran on a ratio of 4 to 1, or about $4,000,000 annually for gold, and four times as much for silver. During this period Colorado was frequently referred to as the "Silver State."

75

IDAHO SPRINGS AND SALIDA WERE BOOMING

Idaho Springs, seat of a major gold discovery in 1859, had a long and prosperous mining life. Here is the Newhouse (later Argo) mill and tunnel which pierced deep under the mountains for five miles to tap mines as far away as Central City. Salida (below) was a busy rail center.

As a natural concomitant. smelting developed on a grand scale to take care of the vast mineral production and was the foundation for a number of new fortunes. The principal centers were Leadville (where the millionaire Guggenheims began), Pueblo, Durango, and Denver. In 1878, the same year he was elected senator, wealthy Nathaniel Hill moved his Black Hawk smelter down to Argo on the outskirts of Denver. His action started the movement to place smelter sites close to coal areas. But in addition to the large centers, smelters were also operating on a lesser scale at places like Golden, Silverton, Lake City, Rico, Tin Cup, Gothic, and Aspen.

Coal production took a surge upward to meet the demand of the railroads for fuel to stoke engines. It rose from 13,500 tons in 1870 to 462,000 in 1880, and by 1890 had made the phenomenal rise to over 3,000,000 tons annually. Associated with the coal story is the manufacture of iron, and when the Colorado Coal and Iron Company (later the Colorado Fuel and Iron) began the construction of a steel plant at Pueblo in 1880, this town took on new stature. During the next decade its population multiplied eight times.

Simultaneous, and perhaps less noteworthy but of solid importance, was the steady rise in agriculture through the building of irrigation ditches. During the decade of the 1880's constant construction was in progress along the South Platte, the Arkansas, and the Rio Grande. On the Platte River the North Poudre Canal, the Larimer County, the Burlington, and the Highline Canals reclaimed 250,000 acres. On the Arkansas the Fort Lyon (the longest ditch in the state—one hundred five miles), the Catlin. the Bessemer, and the Amity Canals were dug, as were four large canals in the San Luis Valley.

The state began to grow magnificent and varied crops—Greeley potatoes and alfalfa in the Platte Valley; and along the Arkansas, the justly famous cantaloupe and Rocky Ford melons. At first the farmers marketed their produce in the many booming mining camps. But as the various localities began to perfect their specialties, marketing was expanded to include shipments outside the state.

The decade of the 1890's dawned bright and clear. Silver production went up to $20,000,000 a year and remained constant for three years, augmented by the startling discovery of another camp. In the spring of 1889 on a branch of the upper Rio Grande, Nicholas C. Creede, an old-time prospector, found some yellow green porphyry protruding through the grass under a large pine high above a canyon. He swung his pick and loosened a specimen.

"Holy Moses!" he exclaimed, "Chloride of silver, by the Holy Moses!"

77

He kept his find more or less secret, working only with a few friends until October, 1890, when he was sure of $70,000 financial backing from David Moffat, Denver banker and president of the Denver and Rio Grande, L. E. Campbell, quartermaster at Fort Logan, and J. J. Brown, husband of the inimitable "Unsinkable" Mrs. Brown. After development started on the vein (which Creede called the Holy Moses mine), the news of his $70,000 sale was out, and another wild stampede followed. By late fall of 1890 there was a settlement, named Creede, in the East Willow Creek canyon far below the location of its Holy Moses mine on the side of Campbell Mountain.

Like so many mining camps before it, the buildings, like Topsy, "just growed." In this instance the pine board shanties were cramped into the narrowest of confines and gradually spread down the creek to its junction with West Willow Creek and then on down another narrow canyon. Finally the town spilled over onto a flat portion of land below the end of the canyon with its two prominent guardian cliffs.

This wider settlement was first called Jimtown and later Lower Creede. Heavy wagons lumbered into camp and dumped all manner of goods on the fresh boardwalks of the sprouting town—everything from mining tools to fresh meat and vegetables. To take care of the camp's madly incoming traffic, in the autumn of 1891 the Denver and Rio Grande completed a spur up the river and into the narrow canyon of Willow Creek. The pandemonium of a full scale rush was being enacted for the "umpteenth" time in Colorado history.

This rush had the wildness of the Leadville and Tin Cup days. By February, 1892, thirty saloons were in full blast, night and day, and the number mounted to seventy-five through the year. Creede attracted a large number of underworld characters, including the bunco artist, Jefferson Randolph Smith, better known as "Soapy" Smith because of his confidence game about hiding money in the wrappers with cakes of soap, twenty-seven-year-old Bob Ford who had treacherously shot Jesse James for a $10,000 reward he never collected, and Bat Masterson who was reputed to have killed twenty-six men in gun duels. All three men ran saloons with gambling rooms. Bob Ford added a variety hall and employed the most notorious girls of the demimonde.

Slanting Annie was the acknowledged queen of the town's many prostitutes, her nickname having been acquired because she was tall and thin and walked bending forward. (Eventually she was buried on the long slope of Bulldog Mountain in the "shot gun" graveyard, so named because everybody buried there had been shot.) Drunken fist fights over the sporting girls occurred almost hourly every night and these

78

THE DIRTY LITTLE COWARD KILLED MR. HOWARD

Bob Ford's funeral brought out all the underworld to the graveyard on the hill. In August, 1892, his widow had him reburied in Missouri.

feuds led to worse violence. In the midst of the sensational disorders of the town, Soapy Smith proclaimed himself dictator of Creede and made it stick. Gamblers and members of the underworld had to pay him tribute and with his own strong-arm methods he controlled what law enforcement there was.

Murders were frequent. The most scandalous was that of Bob Ford who had antagonized a large element of the town by getting drunk and shooting up the place in the spring of 1892. A Citizens Committee was formed to try to wrest control from the underworld, and they warned Ford to leave town as resentment was growing against him and he might be lynched. Ford paid a fine for his spree but refused to leave town.

The situation came to a head in June three days after a fire burned Lower Creede to the ground. Like so many other mining camps before it. Creede was leveled in an agonizingly few hours. These towns, built almost entirely of wood in high mountain areas where water was a problem, were especially vulnerable. Nevadaville had been annihilated in 1861; the business section of Central City in 1874 (to mention only two of many), and now Lower Creede on June 5, 1892. A number of Bob Ford's enemies insinuated he was to blame, and on June 8 he was shot in cold blood by one Edward O'Kelley, who subsequently spent ten years in the penitentiary at Canon City for his crime.

Creede rebuilt in a surprisingly short time, not foreseeing the sure decline of silver and the camp's own death. Although the new mining town's bonanza days were brief, they have lived on, immortalized in Cy Warman's verse:

"IT'S DAY ALL DAY IN THE DAYTIME..."

The upper class of Creede eventually won out. Here is the start of a fishing trip before a quaint house that still stands behind the hotel.

"Here the meek and mild-eyed burros
On mineral mountains feed—
It's day all day in the daytime,
And there is no night in Creede."

At the time of N. C. Creede's first efforts to prove the worth of his discovery by blasting out an eighty-foot shaft in the Holy Moses during July, 1890, Denver was celebrating the Fourth, or Independence Day, in a much quieter manner. The question of a state capital and an adequate building had never been conclusively settled until the late 1880's when the legislature confirmed its decision with an appropriation. On July 4, 1890, the cornerstone for a state capitol building was laid while special ceremonies marked the occasion. A band played, speeches were delivered, and a Masonic choir of one thousand voices sang "The Star-Spangled Banner" for an audience who sat trying to fend off the summer sun with swishing palm-leaf fans and brightly-colored parasols.

Construction of the imposing edifice proved to be slow. The building was not finished until 1900, but was used by the governor and legislature after 1894. It is constructed of grey granite from Gunnison and stands on a hill, donated for the purpose by Henry C. Brown, builder of the Brown Palace Hotel.

While Denverites watched the laying of the capitol's cornerstone, their city was in the midst of a building boom. This boom had begun during the very first years of the 1880's with the erection of the Tabor Block, Windsor Hotel, and Tabor Grand Opera House, and had continued rather steadily. The early 1890's saw the opening of the Broadway Theatre (torn down to erect the Mile High Center), Metropole Hotel (now in 1963 a wing of the Cosmopolitan Hotel), Equitable Building, and Brown Palace Hotel. Prosperity reigned on every side.

But all was not really well. It was only a surface prosperity. Unexpectedly cracks and fissures began to appear in this smooth veneer of apparent well-being. The first Coloradans to run into trouble were the dry farmers on the eastern plains. During the wet years of the 1880's too much grassland was plowed up and too many people settled on questionable farm areas. When the '90's brought three successive seasons of drought, crops shriveled up and soil blew away. The plains were turned into a dry and barren wilderness. People abandoned their farms, many of them seeking relief in Denver and the larger cities.

City life was not the answer. During the optimistic decade just passed, a large majority of business men, as well as farmers, had overexpanded. Debt, extravagance, and speculation had been the order of the day and were now exacting toll. As prices began to decline and economic pressures to tighten, Farmers' Alliances and Workers' Unions were organized in an effort to solve the growing ills.

Colorado's real trouble soon came startlingly to the fore. This was the question of silver, which was being over-produced. The United States government had originally used the system of bi-metallism for its coinage of money and still used both gold and silver for backing paper money. Congress had changed the exact ratio of backing in 1873 and in 1878. In 1890 it had passed the Sherman Silver Purchase Act which further lessened the position of silver but insured that the government would continue as a heavy silver customer. Western Republicans were largely responsible for this policy of government buying.

Ex-President Grover Cleveland, leader of the Democrats, and his Wall Street backers were committed to the gold standard. In 1893, after four years under the Republican president, Benjamin Harrison, Cleveland came back into the presidency. During the winter and spring the price of silver steadily declined, and business across the nation tightened. A depression began to develop everywhere, but particularly in those states in the Rocky Mountains which were dependent on silver mining. By June the price of silver headed down again and in four days catapulted from 83¢ to 62¢ an ounce. Silver mines and their affiliated smelters shut down, unable to operate at a profit, and Colorado was racked by fear.

The gloomy situation reached panic proportions in mid-July. Ten banks in Denver alone failed in three days, and similar failures were

81

THE STATE CAPITOL IS ONE MILE ABOVE SEA LEVEL WITH A GOLD LEAF DOME

The exact spot of 5,280 feet in altitude is carved on one of the stone steps on the highest flight as seen in this photo, looking east from the other end of the civic center. Otto Mears was instrumental in seeing that real gold leaf was used, and the guided tours show his portrait.

repeated throughout the state. Businesses closed and former millionaires, such as Horace Tabor and Jerome Wheeler, whose investments were predominantly in silver mines, went broke. Miners who lost their jobs fled the camps such as Georgetown, Tin Cup, Aspen, and Creede to find work in the gold camps. Thousands of unemployed workers descended on Denver for relief.

To meet the national situation which was at its worst in the summer of 1893, President Cleveland called a special meeting of Congress on August 7 to repeal the Sherman Act (which was regarded by Easterners as the central cause of the panic). Although repeal was valiantly opposed by the Colorado Senators through the next hard-fought months, the motion passed the first of November. Colorado, largest silver producing state in the union, would be hard hit, as the next difficult months were to prove.

Robberies and violence increased throughout the state. These parlous times led to labor difficulties and repeated strikes. The local militia, the National Guard, and Federal troops were called out on successive occasions in the next two years to maintain order or to settle strikes of railroad workers, coal miners, and metal miners. The Populist Party, which had been created in the stress of these difficulties and stood for the free coinage of silver, was swept into power in the confusion. It struggled to maintain order. Colorado would regain equilibrium, the Populist leaders kept repeating, by the restitution of silver.

And true enough, Colorado was actually saved by her mines—not by the silver ones but by the fabulous luck of another gold strike. Gold had first made Colorado; now gold saved her.

This time the gold poured in from Cripple Creek, a new camp back of Pikes Peak. The discovery was made by Bob Womack in most unlikely gravel on a grassy meadow in 1889 after he had prospected for years in the district. At the time he was employed as a cowhand for the Bennett and Myers ranch. He took his ore into Colorado Springs to have specimens assayed, and the report proved the rich worth of his find. Next he tried to get backing to establish where the vein ran and then to start development. He was not very successful but he was able to interest a dentist, John P. Grannis, into grubstaking him to $500 in December. Bob promptly got drunk to celebrate his good fortune.

During 1890 Bob continued to prospect in the Cripple Creek region, trying to establish the type of ore deposits. Nothing much came of his activities, although he did locate the El Paso lode, later called the Gold King, which produced three million dollars up to 1951. Womack and Grannis exhibited a specimen of this ore in a Colorado Springs window

THE BROADMOOR BEGAN AS A CASINO

The Broadmoor had added a dancing pavilion to its gambling activities (which began in 1892) when this photo was taken circa 1907-1910.

at the end of 1890 which started people talking. By January of 1891 a few tenderfeet began drifting into the locality of the Bennett and Myers ranch to look the situation over. During the spring and summer the camp slowly grew to a population of over four hundred, but no find was sufficiently rich to induce capitalists to invest on a large scale. It was not until November that Count James Pourtales of Colorado Springs announced that he and a partner were buying the Buena Vista claim for $80,000. This astounding news created the last and biggest of the Colorado mining stampedes.

Womack, the discoverer, did not get rich as did Nicholas Creede who had started the previous year's rush. He got drunk and threw away his half interest in the Gold King to his partner for $300. Although Womack was cheated out of a reward, his tenacious belief in the Cripple Creek district uncovered the biggest bonanza mines of the state's history and the richest gold camp in the United States.

By 1892 the population had jumped to 2500 and by 1893, to 12,500. In 1894 the camp produced two million dollars in gold and in the next year trebled this sum. The annual amount climbed to seven, to ten, to thirteen, and finally to eighteen million dollars in the year 1900. During the decade after that, the district's average production annually was $15,000,000. No one had ever seen anything like it—its wealth, its excitement, or its affluent red-light district—and all of Colorado profited.

A fresh set of millionaires was created, among them Spencer Penrose, Albert E. Carlton, Charles Tutt, Horace Bennett, and Verner Z. Reed. The most fantastic overnight moneybags was W. S. Stratton, "Midas of the Rockies," as he was called. The eccentric Stratton lived in Colorado

84

WOLHURST WAS A GAY COUNTRY ESTATE

Senator E. O. Wolcott built the original building in the 1890's for lavish houseparties. Later it was owned by wealthy Thomas F. Walsh.

Springs. As his Independence Mine continued to pour out wealth, he developed into a much-discussed character. He was genuinely philanthropic and was responsible for many large and small generosities. One delightful gesture was to give every laundry woman in Colorado Springs a bicycle, equipped with a handlebar basket, so that she would not have to be burdened delivering laundry on foot.

During the late 1890's in the new wave of prosperity engendered by Cripple Creek gold, the silver debacle was forgotten. The United States formally adopted the gold standard in 1900, and no murmur of dissent was heard from Colorado which in the intervening seven years had adjusted its economy to the loss of silver-mining as its main industry.

While those seven years were passing, the Spanish-American War also came and went. Considering that Colorado was so far removed from the hostilities, the state sent a surprising number of volunteers, and one massive benefit for the soldiers was held at the country estate of Senator E. O. Wolcott, south of Littleton.

Ten thousand people attended the prodigious fete, transported on special trains, running from Denver at fifteen-minute intervals all afternoon and evening on the magnificently fair day of August 27, 1898. The grounds were decorated with flags, banners, Chinese lanterns and innumerable festooned tents and elaborate booths (one candy booth being in the shape of the U.S.S. "Colorado"). The coach house was turned into a theatre; the barns into restaurants where French chefs served Parisian dishes. The greatest spectacle took place in the afternoon on a mock battlefield when the 15th infantry, stationed in Denver, routed a much larger force of imitation Spaniards.

AGRICULTURE SUPERSEDED MINING

Mountain-grown hay has always been high in nutriment value and has continued as one of many fine crops produced in diversified farming.

At the turn of the century the state was busy again and was launched on a period of general up-building. As the twentieth century progressed, the focus was less and less on mining, and more and more on agriculture and tourist attractions.

In the forefront of agriculture was the newly-launched sugar beet industry. Its first factory had been put into operation at Grand Junction in 1899 to take care of small crops of beets begun as early as 1873. Around the turn of the century, Charles Boettcher, who was one of the early Leadville millionaires, made a visit to his native Germany. He heard about the beet sugar industry there and was told that the beets thrived with good soil and sunshine.

"Colorado has plenty of both," he replied and bought some seed to bring home to Colorado farmers. Platte valley experimentation proved that the beets would yield a large sugar content in that area. Enormous acreages were turned over to sugar beets and six plants were opened in towns northeast of Denver. Boettcher and his friends supplied the backing. In 1905 these plants were amalgamated into a corporation called the Great Western Sugar Company which has prospered ever since.

The state had always been famous for its scenery. Many nineteenth-century visitors had publicized the wonders to be viewed in Colorado in later travel books and reminiscences. Yet Colorado had rather ignored the potentiality. Now the natives began to see the business possibilities in acting as commercial hosts and to look about them at the grandeur in their mountains with a different viewpoint. An interest in tourists required that more attention be given to the forests, which were fast being denuded, and to the preservation of wild animals and game, in danger of disappearing.

HORSES AND FIELD HANDS HARVESTED SUGAR

Originally the sugar beet industry required an enormous amount of hand labor but in recent years has become increasingly mechanized.

President Theodore Roosevelt, a great lover of the outdoors, was in the vanguard of a growing public opinion for *conservation*, a brand-new term in the thinking of the day. He had made a number of trips to Colorado in the early 1900's, hunting antelope on the eastern plains and bear and cougar on the Western Slope. "T.R." knew the conditions at first hand and under his leadership a number of national forests were created. Plans for other conservation and reclamation projects gained momentum. If Colorado was to attract visitors, the inhabitants would have to refrain from despoiling the scenery. If the state was to continue to have an expanding population, it would have to exploit every means to feed its people.

One of the earliest undertakings of the newly created U. S. Reclamation Service was the Uncompahgre project which called for the building of a nearly six-mile tunnel under Vernal Mesa to carry water from the Black Canyon of the Gunnison to the Uncompaghre valley. Here there was rich land for growing fruit and other fine crops but insufficient water. The crews began boring from each side of the mesa in 1905 and met in 1909. President William Howard Taft made a much-touted trip to Colorado and over the mountains to Montrose where on September 23 he threw the switch and sent leaping gallons of water flowing through the tunnel to add to Colorado's prosperity and beauty.

But not all was beautiful after the turn of the century—there was ugliness, too. Labor troubles flared again and led to strikes and violence in many of the mining camps. The most serious disturbance occurred at Cripple Creek where 3,500 men struck in 1903 and continued to agitate for nearly a year. The National Guard was called out. Eventually a dynamite trap to catch an incoming train bearing "scabs" was set under

DAVID MOFFAT

The great railroad man, banker, miner and builder, is standing beside the first train down Gore Canyon. Moffat eventually went broke, sinking his millions in an effort to complete a transcontinental line through Colorado. The Moffat Tunnel was his dream and memorial.

the depot platform with a devilish scheme for detonation. Thirteen non-union men were killed. This act lost the strike and swayed public opinion to the mine owners' side. The strike leaders were rounded up, placed in railroad cars, deported to Kansas or New Mexico, and warned not to return. It was a case of injustice and cruelty on both sides.

From 1910 forward, the history of the state takes on a complexity impossible to cover in a short summary. Colorado fell off as a mining state and rose as an agricultural and industrial state. Agriculture developed a number of unique products such as Pascal celery, pink-meated cantaloupes from around Rocky Ford (instead of the original Netted Gem variety with green meat), and the fragrant and variegated Colorado carnations. The latter are now flown regularly to the East and to Europe.

The industrial activity led to one of the most shameful episodes in the state's roster. This was the Ludlow Massacre, which occurred in 1914 at a coal field eighteen miles north of Trinidad. For months, during a prolonged strike of fields in Colorado, the eastern press blazoned the grisly details of the battle between Capital and Labor. Both sides sent in out-of-state forces, and the contest developed into a minor Spanish Civil War in that it was a test case for a larger struggle to come. Spain served as a proving ground for the forces of Communism against those

BULLY "T. R."

President Roosevelt is shown on the unique over-hanging bridge in the Royal Gorge in May, 1905, after his hunting trip out from Glenwood Springs. Hopping up is Skip, the terrier, that captivated "T.R." on the hunt and was taken back to the White House.

of Fascism while each side sent into the country outside supplies of men and ammunition. In Colorado the same thing occurred as union forces lined up against management and each side sent in battlers from beyond the state's borders.

Strikers wanted their union, the United Mine Workers, recognized in the state's southern coal fields of the Trinidad area and in the northern coal fields of Boulder County. They also wanted an increase in wages and the abolition of numerous abuses. Colorado mining laws prohibited these abuses, but they were unenforced by the mine owners. County sheriffs were bought off, safety regulations were ignored, and the number of fatalities was appalling. It was claimed that five hundred miners lost their lives in Las Animas County alone because of inadequate safety precautions.

Chief offender was the Colorado Fuel and Iron Company, which in 1912 was largely owned by Rockefeller interests and controlled the southern fields. The company not only owned the mines, but the houses and stores as well, and forced the workers to patronize only company-owned facilities.

On September 23, 1913, twelve thousand strikers moved out of company-owned houses at the various coal fields and into their own tents. The coal operators armed guards at the mines and imported thugs to

89

IRRIGATION

Ditches made growing fruit trees possible on the Western Slope; here, at the Palisades near Grand Junction.

intimidate the workers. In the next month clashes multiplied, and beatings and murders occurred, particularly in the southern group. Each side denounced the other, but the coal operators had the ear of important newspaper publishers. The local press blamed the union leaders.

Governor E. M. Ammons called out the National Guard and implied that the troops were there to deal with the striking miners. The Guard used strong-arm methods and searched the strikers' tents without warrants, looking for weapons. Armed employees of the mine owners were recruited directly into the National Guard. During the winter, as trouble heightened into a warlike belligerence in Las Animas and Huerfano Counties, the Guard ceased to be a neutral force to maintain law and order for the state of Colorado. It became a tool of the mine owners.

The largest tent colony was at Ludlow, where about nine hundred men, women, and children were housed. On April 20, 1914, the Guard ruthlessly attacked the tent camp and killed six men, two women, and eleven children, besides maiming many others. Public opinion rebelled at once, and a national scandal resulted.

A Congressional investigation was held, and the National Guard was publicly condemned. President Woodrow Wilson was asked to handle the situation. The United States army moved in, disarmed everyone— strikers and guards alike. It set up a rigid barricade against any further importation into the state of men or weapons and quickly restored order.

A number of needed reforms resulted from this tragic affair, although technically Labor lost at the time. The strike petered out and the union failed of recognition. But in the succeeding years John D. Rockefeller, Jr., made a personal investigation in Colorado and reorganized the worker-management set-up of the C. F. and I., while the state created an Industrial Commission with power to investigate and remedy hazardous working conditions. The final result was good and a definite step forward for Labor whose gains were finally solidified in 1927, after a second tragic strike against the Rocky Mountain Fuel Company in Weld County.

PRESIDENT

Taft made a speech at Montrose as part of the ceremonies attending the opening of the Gunnison water tunnel.

Throughout the next decades the state's history paralleled that of the nation with only a few deviations.

During World War I mining fell away all over the state with the exception of the tungsten mines in Boulder County. But they, too, died at the close of the war. Eventually the discovery of one enormous deposit of molybdenum on Bartlett Mountain at Climax kept the state's mining figures up. But mostly Colorado's greatest industry was on the downgrade.

The 1920's were characterized by the same advances and madnesses that gripped the whole United States. In the 1930's, following a usual twenty-year cycle, another drought blighted the dry farms of the plains area and wreaked enormous damage. This made the intensity of the depression more dismal than in any other place in the union with the exception of those states which also had an excess of dry-farming. Colorado's depression on the plains was characterized by gulleyed, hideous soil erosion and black, cutting, and swirling dust storms that traveled as far westward as Denver.

In the mountains the bleak years were different, too. When the depression caused President Roosevelt, acting under the authority of the Gold Reserve Act of January, 1934, to devalue the dollar, the price of gold jumped from $20 to $35 an ounce. A renascence occurred for Colorado's gold-mining camps. Places like Central City and Cripple Creek awoke from a ghost-like quiet. Unemployed men flocked into the gulches to pan and sluice gold, and others opened up abandoned mines. During the next few years they were lively spots again, but subsided when the miners were drafted for a second World War.

The World War II period saw a marked rise in the use of Colorado as an aviation center because of its many sunny days and its high altitude. A number of air force training camps were built within the state's borders, and success of these camps focused national attention on Colorado. In the post-war years, commercial airlines chose Denver for their

˙TWO TRAGEDIES OF THE TWENTIETH CENTURY

Above Red Cross workers are searching the ruins of the Ludlow tent colony, after the infamous attack, April 12, 1914, killing nineteen people. Below starving unemployed men, in the 1930's depression, try their hand at panning gold in Denver. Many recovered $2 a day.

*   *   *

On the opposite page the original ski jump at Steamboat Springs, built by Carl Howelsen in 1911, is above. He was a Norwegian stone mason who inspired the town with the sport. Below are the mountains of Aspen with three ski areas on Aspen, Highland and Buttermilk.

THE OLDEST AND BIGGEST SKI RESORTS

THE OLD

Faithful burros and a shepherd dog were part of the equipment for prospecting long ago.

headquarters, and in 1954 the U. S. Air Force picked a site north of Colorado Springs for its air academy.

Another post-war development was the rise of ski resorts, which stretched the business of entertaining visitors over two seasons. Winter Park, Berthoud, Arapahoe Basin, Loveland, Aspen, Steamboat Springs, and Hidden Valley in Estes were only a few of many tourist places that installed new tows and chair lifts or added more lodges and hotels.

Manufacturing rose in the late 1940's, and two of the most sensational developments of the post-war era in Colorado were the discovery of new oil fields and deposits of uranium. Suddenly the cry was everywhere: "Uranium!" and tenderfeet were scrambling over the mountains as madly as in the nineteenth century. The excitement brought the temper of the state full circle.

A century ago the cry was "gold," and everyone was feverishly searching for it. In the 1950's it was "oil" or "uranium," and again hordes of prospectors swarmed the countryside. It was the same old story—unusual enterprise, fantastic luck, wild delusions, jumped claims, litigation, stock speculation, crooked promotion, and overnight millionaires (such as Charles Steen and Vernon Pick). All were here again. Colorado's dramatic terrain had the habit of creating dramatic and violent history, and the only difference seemed to be that the new prospectors set off with a jeep instead of a burro.

Toward the end of the decade Colorado chose to celebrate its one hundredth birthday in 1959. This was just one hundred years after the first pell-mell rush to find gold following Green Russell's discovery of a placer in Little Dry Creek during July of the year before. The state decided to call its festivities the Rush-to-the-Rockies Centennial and planned a series of world championship contests, national sporting

THE NEW

*With uranium pros-
pectors, they re-
quired a jeep and
a Geiger counter —
but still a dog!*

events, national conventions for square dancers, educators and the like, exhibits, concerts, plays, pageants, rodeos, jeep tours, burro races, festivals and fiestas that would adequately commemorate the passage of a hundred years.

True, the state's first permanent settlements in the San Luis Valley passed their century birthdays in 1951, '52 and '53; while February, 1961, marks the one hundredth anniversary of Colorado Territory as such. But the state, as a white man's home, was considered to be in 1959 a round century old.

The Colorado mountains, which raise their snow-capped rampart against a fair blue sky, are aeons old. It is these hills and peaks with their ageless granite calm and the vast sweep of the limitless plains that have created the fantastic events of the many past centuries. They dwarf completely the pretentions of the white man to his own history—however strange and chaotic it may have been in the last hundred-odd years, or however magical has been the progress in that time from ox-drawn covered Conestogas and six-horse Concord stagecoaches to diesel-engined streamliners and jet-propelled airplanes. The white man is still a comparative newcomer to those prairies and peaks.

So there the state proudly stands: the highest rampart of the nation, ever red, every rosy, ever colorful — Colorado.

*   *   *

Credits for Illustrations